a

LONDON BOROUGH OF LEWISHAM
LIBRARY SERVICE

Author

Title

Books or discs must be returned on or before the last date stamped on label or on card in book pocket. Books or discs can be renewed by telephone, letter or personal call unless required by another reader. After library hours use the Ansafone Service (01-698 7347). For hours of opening and charges see notices at the above branch, but note that all lending departments close a   pm on Wednesday and all libraries are closed on Sundays, Good Friday, Christmas Day, Bank Holidays and Saturdays prior to Bank Holidays

CASTLE AND TOWN

THE EARTHEN MOUND

Frontispiece

CASTLE AND TOWN

CHAPTERS IN THE HISTORY OF
THE ROYAL BURGH OF EDINBURGH

BY

DAVID ROBERTSON, M.A.
DEPUTE TOWN CLERK

AND

MARGUERITE WOOD, Ph.D.

OLIVER AND BOYD
EDINBURGH: TWEEDDALE COURT
LONDON: 33 PATERNOSTER ROW, E.C.
1928

PREFACE

THERE are so many books about Edinburgh that some explanation seems necessary for an addition to their number.

It is easy to find the part played by the city in national history, and many people have written about the famous men who frequented its streets, indeed about the very stones of the streets. Yet there is something left untold.

We are apt to take the present for granted, without considering how the customs, institutions, and privileges which we enjoy came to be. The city has grown within the memory of most of us, but many important changes belong to the life of past generations. To take one comparatively slight instance, how many know how we came to possess the gardens which are the beauty of Princes Street? Some may still remember when entrance to them was a coveted privilege, but there must be many who do not know the stages by which they came to replace that old defence of the town, the North Loch.

So it is with the other chapters. They attempt to recount the ways by which the city came to enjoy the position which it now holds, and to set

Preface

the stage upon which so much of the history of Scotland was enacted.

The materials for these chapters have been obtained from the records and miscellaneous papers in the City Chambers, which are in the charge of Miss Wood. They profess to state the official point of view, as disclosed in the records, and in this respect they may convey impressions which fall to be supplemented, perhaps in some instances to be corrected, from other sources. Mr Robertson has written chapters I., II., III., IV., VII., and IX., and Miss Wood chapters V., VI., VIII., X., and XI.

CITY CHAMBERS,
EDINBURGH, *November* 1928.

CONTENTS

ix

LIST OF ILLUSTRATIONS

CASTLE AND TOWN

CHAPTER I

THE NORTH LOCH

IT has been said that Princes Street is the finest street in Europe, and while there may be other claimants for this distinction it is still the case that Princes Street enjoys a world-wide fame, which partly is owing to the grandeur of the Castle Rock and partly to the picturesque valley which lies between the new town and the old. This valley is laid out as ornamental garden ground, and so greatly is it valued by the citizens that nothing short of legal compulsion would induce them to surrender any portion of it. The prosperity of the city depends in a peculiar degree upon the attractions it offers to the visitors who come from all parts of the world and to the large number of persons who make choice of Edinburgh as their place of residence. It follows that any proposal which seems to threaten or affect the Princes Street Gardens is bound to create a lively interest on the part of the citizens. Proposals of this nature have inevitably arisen at different times, and have been the occasion of controversies which are now forgotten, but one may read about them in the old books and papers stored in the City Chambers. It may not be out of place to set down some of the information to be found in those old records, and incidentally to bring together some passages of history connected with the Princes Street Gardens which have not hitherto appeared in narrative form.

The valley which interposes between the new town and the old has been hollowed out by glacier action in one of the epochs known to students of geology as an ice period, which is not regarded as remote, but as recent in the sense of that science. Mr Henry Cadell, in his book *The Story of the Forth*, gives an interesting map of this locality at the time of the 25-feet beach, showing some six or seven lochs in and about Edinburgh, including one at Holyrood and also a small stream rising in the vicinity of St Cuthbert's and running through the valley down to the loch at Holyrood. This is a statement of probabilities only, and as it happens both loch and stream have now disappeared. Perhaps the small sheet of water known as St Margaret's Loch is a relic of the Holyrood Loch shrivelled and dried up with age; and the sewer which runs through the Princes Street Gardens towards Holyrood may be the lineal successor of the stream shown by Mr Cadell. In historic times, that is when the Castle Rock was being occupied as a fortress and the burgh was taking shape, the valley contained pools of water and wide morasses covered with tangled woods

The King's Garden

and haunted by wild animals. Maitland, in his book about Edinburgh, states that the place which came to be occupied by the North Loch was formerly a dry bottom with no other water therein than a very small stripe or rill arising from the two wells or springs issuing out of the Castle Rock with some springs in the ground to the north. "That that little vale," he writes, "was anciently a dry bottom is attested by Walter Bowmaker, Abbot of Inchcolm in the Firth of Forth, and continuer of Fordun's Chronicle, who tells us that the Queen in the year 1398 appointed a tournament of twelve knights of whom David Stewart, the prince her son, was the chief to be held in a place adjoining to the northern side of the town of Edinburgh where the loch is at present." Some centuries before the date mentioned, probably in the reign of King David I., the valley had dried up, or more probably had been drained and planted and had become the King's Garden and a pleasaunce for the accommodation of the royal household. Cosmo Innes, in his book on early Scottish history, mentions that King David had a dwelling on the rock and a garden on the bank between it and the Church of St Cuthbert. In the original Charter of Holyrood the King makes a reference to the well which "springeth near the corner of my garden by the way which leads to the Church of St Cuthberts." In this garden St David budded trees and cultivated such fruits and flowers as were then known in Scotland. At this remote period, therefore, and apparently for about three centuries afterwards, the valley is said to have been devoted to the peaceful function which it now fulfils, but there is no record or history to provide us with any details.

It was in the reign of King James II. that the North Loch was first projected and formed. The King deemed it necessary to forego the pleasures of his garden in order to ensure the safety of the town, which was continually being threatened by the old enemies of England. The gardens were therefore destroyed, and in their place a loch was substituted which extended from the Castle Rock to the line of the Netherbow. Grant in his history states that in 1450, after the battle of Sark in which the English were defeated with great slaughter, the city was enclosed by a wall, scarcely any trace of which now remains, except the picturesque old ruin known as the Wellhouse Tower at the base of the Castle Rock. It had been intended to defend the north side of the town by a fosse or moat, but the water coming from the well at the base of the Castle Rock was so abundant that a permanent loch was formed. The wall ran along the southern declivity of the ridge on which the old town was built, between the High Street and the Cowgate, then crossed the ridge at the Netherbow and terminated at the east end of the loch. For another period of three centuries the valley was occupied by the North Loch, its main purpose being to protect the town, which it did very

A Defence of the Town

effectively, so that in the unhappy wars from which the country was never free throughout the reigns of successive Stuart Kings, those enemies who entered the city did so from the south and not from the north side. According to Gordon of Rothiemay's map (1647), the Flodden wall descended along the west side of Leith Wynd, enclosed the Trinity College Church and ended at the foot of the North Loch, where a dam and sluice or "clows" regulated the waters. In Edgar's Map, which is 100 years later in date than Gordon's Map, the waters of the North Loch came no farther eastward than the line of the future North Bridge, between which and the Trinity Hospital there lay the old Physic Gardens. At the time of the Jacobite rising of 1715 the Magistrates caused the sluice of the loch to be completely dammed up to let the water rise, but no such precautions for the safety of the town were taken in 1745. Shortly after the date of the second rising, when this form of defence had lost its importance, the loch was drained and reduced to a quarter of the area it had originally occupied.

The North Loch comes prominently into the history of old Edinburgh, and since it was part of the town's property there are numerous references to it in the Burgh Records. A sheet of water lying under the shadow of a great rock could not fail to be picturesque, and probably, viewed from a distance, the North Loch was a thing of beauty,

The Town Council and the North Loch.

with the Trinity College at its eastern shore and the glebe and church of St Cuthbert at its western shore. On the north the ground rose quickly and was cultivated by the farmer of Loch-bank or Bearford's Parks. A model of the old town in the reign of Queen Mary may be seen in the City Museum, and it shows the loch as ornamented with pleasure boats and swans. The gardens of the houses sloped downwards from the High Street and Lawnmarket to the edge of the water; for example, Lady Stair's house had a terraced garden descending in this way. But the conception of amenity is of recent date and was non-existent in the Edinburgh of the Stuart Kings, and the impression remains that the loch unfortunately was made a receptacle for all kinds of refuse and impurity and chiefly tenanted by water-rats and eels.

On 14th February 1499-1500, the Town Council ordained that in time of pest the cleansing should be at the running Water of Leith and no other place, "nor yet at the south loch, nor yet at the North Loch."

On 6th July 1554 the Treasurer was ordained "to make ane clowse," that is a sluice, at the east end of the North Loch, "for halding in of ye watter yrof." This subject is mentioned at different times; thus, on 25th November 1573, an order was given "to dam and had in the North Loch to the umest house." The sluice was so formed that it could be manipulated to raise or lower the water and in this way to increase or decrease the area over which it extended. On 16th October 1556, it was ordained that the fleshers and slayers of cattle, sheep and swine, and the "users of issues thairof," should cause carry the filth of the same to the North Loch. It will be remembered that in 1558 the Reformers ducked the effigy of St Giles in the North Loch, no doubt at the place where a pillar and basin were provided for dealing with offenders against the seventh commandment, "whilk rased na small truble in the toun." On 4th September 1584, the Town Council arranged to pass and visit the eel ark at the east end of the North Loch. This eel ark was at one time let to a tenant who was taken bound to feed the swans on the loch. In March 1598-9 it was let on a five years' tack to Alexander Adamson for a rent of 50 merks. On 2nd December 1601, mention is made of the loss sustained by the tacksman of the eel ark, through letting out the water of the loch, and five merks were remitted from his rent for the year. The loch must have abounded in eels in these early days, for Nicoll records that in February 1655, in consequence of stormy weather, some thousands of them were cast upon its banks "to the admiration of many." In the old taverns the dishes served up to patrons included eel-pie and North Loch trout.

The swans on the loch are referred to in a variety of Minutes. Thus, on 8th December 1589, a payment of 50s. is recorded for oats for the swans on the loch; and similar outlays appear in later years. On 3rd December 1600, the Masters of the Trinity Hospital were required to provide a boll of oats for the swans in the coming winter. On 8th December 1589 there is an interesting reference to an individual accused of shooting a swan from a window in his house which looked out on the loch, and it is stated that other householders had indulged in this form of sport. The person referred to was taken bound to replace the swan he had destroyed and forbidden to shoot from his dwelling-house at any kind of bird on the loch.

In April 1569 a sum of £54, confiscated from William Smith and his wife Black Meg, hanged for concealing the pest, was given to Adam Fullertoun, bailie, to spend on the wall at the North Loch and the well at the Well Tower.

From time to time schemes were suggested in respect of the North Loch. On 7th October 1552, the Minutes refer to a proposal put before the Town Council to bring the Water of Leith into the North Loch, and the scheme was represented as very advantageous to the town and of little expense. On 25th July 1593, an Italian merchant, named Marques, made a more attractive proposal to the Town Council, which was to bring the sea into the loch and to make the water at the shore a fathom deeper, and this was sent for consideration to a Committee of the Town Council, where it was lost.

Plans for Extension

These proposals may seem extravagant but they were repeated and discussed in later years apparently quite seriously. Thus in 1728 the Earl of Mar propounded a scheme whereby a branch of the Water of Leith might be brought from somewhere about Coltbridge to fill and run through the North Loch, "which would be to the great advantage of the convenience, beauty, cleanliness and healthiness of the town." The subject was revived when the Union Canal was projected, towards the close of the eighteenth century, certain of the plans including a continuation through the bed of the North Loch, where a street was formed and actually called Canal Street as will be narrated below.

It was seriously proposed to carry the canal to Greenside, in the area of which an immense harbour was to have been constructed. This again being connected by a broad canal with the sea, it was expected that the new town would thereby be converted into a seaport and the unhappy traders of Leith compelled either to abandon their traffic or to join in with Edinburgh by a premature process of amalgamation. Daniel Wilson states that, chimerical as this project may now appear, designs were furnished by experienced engineers, a map of the whole plan was engraved on a large scale, and the civic reformers rejoiced in the anticipation of seeing the shipping of the chief ports of Europe crowding into the heart of their new capital. The mention of these extraordinary conceptions has, however, interrupted the early history of the North Loch.

A great number of legends and traditions have gathered round the North Loch, many of them recalling its use as a place of public punishment. It was the haunt of all sorts of idle people, and a place of amusement for the citizens, who crowded to its shores when any unfortunate victim of the law was brought thither for a "dookin." In 1562 the Town Council enacted that "alle sic folke as be fund guiltie of notour adulterie or anything that offends the law of God sall be dookit in the North Loch twa times frae the pillar and stule be the lochside." The water attained an average depth of about eight feet, and there was one deep pool of fifteen feet called the "Pot," near to the site of the present Post Office, which used to attract suicides as the Dean Bridge was wont to do in more recent times. In old Scots literature references were common "to tak a dook in the Pot," this being the last remedy for mortal ills. The stule or beam corresponded to the English cucking-stool, and it was erected at the lower end near to the dam or sluice at Halkerston's Wynd, and there it stood and served its purpose for about a hundred years. Women who led a loose life were put here "on ye beame owre ye water"; men were thrown in with a rope attached to the waist and dragged

The Loch as a Place of Punishment.

along the water edge by the mob who gathered to bait the victims. Gradually the loch became the place of punishment for minor as well as major offences, for example being "a scolding wife" or a profane swearer.

In the year 1595 the Town Council decreed that a woman, Jean Tait, should be ducked for speaking scandalous words of one of the town ministers, and it is mentioned that "sixe of the toon men were needed at the dookin." For their services they received twelve pennies Scots apiece, which outlay the woman had afterwards to refund. In another case, which occurred in the beginning of the seventeenth century, a man Sinclair and his sister were placed in a large chest, in the sides of which holes were drilled, and the box was thrown upon the loch in presence of a multitude of people. When the bed of the loch came to be drained in more recent times, there was discovered deeply embedded in the mud at the bottom a huge chest which, on being opened, was found to contain two skeletons, those of a man and a woman, and little doubt was entertained that they were the remains of this unfortunate couple.

In 1609 two individuals, James Martin and William Hart, meal merchants at the Tron, were suspected of adulterating their goods and giving short weight to their customers. After sundry complaints which produced no remedy, their booth was one morning invaded by an angry mob, and, before

11

the merchants well knew what was wrong, their krame was sacked and both of them were dragged to the loch, where a rope was fastened round their waists and the mob "dookit thame thryse, thereafter bade thame goe in peis."

Pitcairn records an instance where a woman was ducked for being " sae dour " as to refuse to do any household work for her husband. The woman was known as Dame Jarlies. The indignity in her case worked no cure, as shortly afterwards she was brought before the Court for assaulting her husband in his sleep.

One of the most curious legends connected with the loch is the case of Betty Trot. She was a hawker and had a little stall in the Lawnmarket for odds - and - ends, and she took charge of the interests of the hawkers in the town and used to boast of the influence she exerted over the Provost David Aitkenhead and other members of the Town Council, before whom she appeared frequently to beg some favour for herself or her fraternity. But about 1635 she fell into disgrace, at the time a fire took place in the Lawnmarket when some jewellery disappeared rather mysteriously. Betty was suspected and searched ; the stolen articles were found in her person, and for her offence she was condemned to be ducked four times in the North Loch as a lesson "to ken the differ between what was her ain geare and ither folks." But according to the narrative Betty was not to be "dookit" without a struggle.

Ducking Offenders

When the public hangman laid hands on her, presumably to tie her to the stool, she knocked him down with one blow so that he fell head over heels into the water. Betty nimbly ran along the bank to where a boat was moored, untied it and was gone almost before the spectators knew what had happened. Two or three other boats started in pursuit and caught her up, but so often as they tried to board her craft Betty made it swing and oscillate so that more than one of them fell into the water amidst the roars of the onlookers. At last she was surrounded and obliged to surrender. Accordingly she held up her hands and permitted three or four of the town officers to enter so as to take hold of her. No sooner, however, did she get them all on board than suddenly she threw all her weight on one side, with the result that the boat turned over and the entire crew was thrown into the water. By the time all of them were safely fished out and brought ashore Betty was deemed to have been ducked enough.

Instances of ducking occurred down to 1660, but became rare about this time. About the year 1663 a woman, Margaret Robb, was drowned while being ducked for some trivial offence and the practice was stopped by order of the Scots Estates. By 1685 the beam and stool had become so rotten and so knocked about through being made a plaything of boys and youths that they were removed, and duckings then ceased altogether.

The North Loch

Among other old memories, one which has a morbid interest is the part played by the North Witchcraft and Suicides. Loch during the period of the persecution of witches. King James VI. may be credited with ushering in this period, and one of his many titles was the "Hammer of the Witches." He wrote a book on Demonology, which became the accepted standard of ideas on the subject, especially in this part of the country, so that Edinburgh earned an evil reputation, and it is said that more witches were "worryit" on the Castle Hill than in all the rest of Scotland. In the trial of persons suspected of intercourse with Satan and the powers of evil there was a preliminary stage known as the ordeal, which frequently took the form of a "dookin." The suspected person, generally an old woman, had her thumbs and toes tied together and was flung into the loch. If she floated that was proof positive of guilt; if she sank that was presumptive proof of innocence ; while if she was drowned outright her innocence was completely vindicated, though this came too late to be of any avail to the poor victim.

A number of cases are given in an old print in the City Chambers. Thus, it is mentioned that in 1589 an old woman, by name Elsie Peat, was subjected to the ordeal of "dookin." She apparently from the infirmity of her age was given to muttering to herself and speaking to children. Suspicion lighted on her and she was flung into the loch, and,

14

through her clothing buoying her up, she floated on the surface for a time, whereupon shouts of horror arose, the mob demanding that she should be "worryit" for a witch. So the poor creature was led to the Castlehill and there burned alive.

In 1592 seven persons, reputed wizards and witches, were put through the ordeal of water in the North Loch. All of them were found guilty and were afterwards burned on the Castlehill. One of the victims was Euphemia M'Calzean, a young lady of good family, who was accused of consorting with the devil and raising a storm with intent to sink the ship in which Anne of Denmark was being conveyed to this country. King James put the blame for this storm upon a number of persons and would listen to no reason in the case of the unfortunate lady, who rather oddly had pretended by way of jest to be a witch. She was cast into the loch, found to be guilty and burned with others at the Castle Hill.

Passing on to a later time, we read that on 15th October 1656 seven wizards and witches were executed in Edinburgh, of whom, says Nicoll, two were burned and five were drowned in the North Loch. It appears that these people had formed a conspiracy against the Commonwealth and had carried it on under the guise of witchcraft. They had bound themselves to deny the lord, meaning Cromwell, and to swear fealty to the black king, meaning Charles. Their actions exposed them to risks in any case, but the authorities chose to construe their conduct according to the letter and not the spirit, and to punish them for witchcraft. The sentences were carried out in presence of an immense company of spectators, many of whom showed their hatred of the supposed witches by yelling and hooting.

Other instances might be given down to the year 1670 when public feeling on this subject began to undergo a change. The evil force of the superstition was slowly dispelled, and from about 1670 the persecution of witches seems to have been abandoned.

From the earliest times of its existence the loch appears to have been regarded by suicides as a convenient place for putting off this mortal coil. Arnot estimated that, from the beginning of the sixteenth century until the middle of the eighteenth, upwards of 150 persons were drowned in its waters, of whom the greater proportion were suicides. Some of these events are mentioned in old histories and some have formed the themes of songs and ballads. Those who were "crazed with grief or crossed in hopeless love" had only to take a "dook in the Pot" to find a respite from their sorrows. There is no lack of legendary matter here, but there is only space to mention one or two well-known cases.

In the year 1707, Robert Balfour, Master of Burleigh, moved by a most unaccountable malice, came to the town of Inverkeithing on horseback and

Old Church of St Cuthbert's

in arms, and having inquired for Henry Stenhouse, schoolmaster there, he challenged him to a duel; and upon the schoolmaster refusing to fight the Master pulled out a pistol and shot him twice, so that he died after languishing for some days. The Master had to stand trial for this crime, and was adjudged to be beheaded at the Cross of Edinburgh on 6th January 1710. He escaped, however, out of the Tolbooth, but was discovered in Leith and again put in prison. A second time he got free, but an alarm was raised and his pursuers made up on him at the North Loch. It was dusk at the time, so crying out that he preferred death to captivity he plunged into the "Pot." He was an expert swimmer and swam under the water for a considerable distance before he rose for breath. In the darkness he was unperceived and got clear away, though it was believed for some time that he had been drowned.

Another incident relates to a shoemaker who proceeded down to the loch intending to drown himself and commenced to wade out where the water was shallow. A number of people witnessed this rash act and began to vent cries of alarm, hearing which the father of Lord Henderland threw up the window of his house in St James' Court, and leaning out, cried down the brae to the people, "What's all the noise about? Canna ye e'en let the honest man gang tae the deil his ain gait?"

In another case, a woman who had resolved to drown herself waded into the water, meaning to take the plunge where the loch was deep enough. As she got out from the shore her hoop caught the water and lifted her off her feet. At the same time the wind caught and blew her willy-nilly away from the bank, which alarmed her so that she screamed for help and waved her arms distractedly. Her cries speedily brought a crowd to the shore, who made preparations to go to her assistance, but before this could be accomplished she had landed in safety on the other side.

In December 1600 the Town Council Minutes make reference to negotiations with Mr John

St Cuthbert's Glebe and Lochbank. Dalzell, who was litigating with them in the Court of Session in regard to the loch, the question being the right of the Town Council to inhold the water and consequently to flood Dalzell's lands, which were at the west end of the loch. The waters were let out so that the bounds of Dalzell's land might be examined ; and in June 1601 an interesting Minute mentions that the dispute between the town and Dalzell was to be submitted amicably to the Lords of Session when the King was present. In May 1601 an agreement was reached by which the town paid Dalzell a sum of £225. This was one of many litigations in which the town came to be involved over the lands around the North Loch.

The Discharge of John Dalzell is still preserved, and in it he describes himself as heritable feuar of "all and sundrie the Kirklands and gleib of ye

New Bridge and Site of the North Loch

Bounds of the Loch

parroche Kirk of St Cuthbert under ye castel wall."
The payment referred to was for the heritable title
and right of an acre and a quarter of the said Kirklands lying within and east of the march stones
which divided the remainder of the Kirklands from
the lands of the North Loch. These march stones
were arranged by a formal ratification, which referred
again to the Kirklands lying on the east side of the
Kirkyard, which property had been annexed to the
Crown and formerly belonged to the vicarage of
St Cuthbert's in the regality of Broughton. The
Agreement narrates that the profits of four acres of
these lands had been lost to Dalzell in consequence
of the building of a wall at the east end of the
North Loch which had raised the level of the water;
and it details the position of the march stones which
divided the Kirklands from the lands pertaining to
the "guid toun" on the east side thereof.

In reference to St Cuthbert's, it may be of
interest to state that in the year 1599 there was a
formal designation of a manse and glebe, and in
the document several familiar names occur, such as
Alexander Fairlie of Braid and Mr Robert Pont,
minister of the church. The manse was a new
house built by Pont, and with its yards it occupied
the area between the common passage to the Kirkyard on the east (part of which still exists, entering
from Princes Street opposite to Charlotte Street)
and the common "gait" that passes to the Water of
Leith on the west, which now is known as King's

The North Loch

Stables Road. The glebe extended to four acres and lay adjacent to the North Loch and to the manse and its yards. A reference to the maps of the area as it was a hundred years ago will show the passage to the churchyard from Princes Street, which skirted the east end of the church and thence proceeded between the two manses, coming out at King's Stables Road.

The Kirklands were sold in 1621 to John Byres of Coats, and in the conveyance there is reserved and excluded the meadow land disponed to the town and the glebe possessed by the minister. In 1716 the Kirklands are mentioned as belonging to Robert Hepburn of Bearford.

In February 1606 the grass at the west end of the loch was let for £5 to one Ninian Macmorane, brother of Bailie John Macmorane. This grass continued to be let out down to the early years of the nineteenth century, and from time to time march stones were placed to mark off the bounds of the town's property. Thus, in February 1661, certain councillors were appointed to visit the march stones of the "lang gaitt" and North Loch head and cause set in stones where they are wanting.

In May 1663 certain councillors were appointed to view the passage lately made at the head of the North Loch by which "wynes and strong wateris" were privily carried in the night time, that if need be a large ditch might be made to impede the transport of these commodities at unlawful times. There are many references to the smuggling of "uncustomed" goods over the loch either by boats or by fords where the water was shallow.

In February 1698 the Town Council received a petition from one Ferguson, a tanner burgess, who had an interest in some slaughter-houses and tanholes lying contiguous to the south side of the loch, which were put under water by the stopping of the sluice. The Town Council ordained the sluice to be opened that the loch might be let out till it fell 10 or 12 inches so that the houses of the petitioner might be habitable.

In June 1702 there occurs an early reference to Robert Hepburn of Bearford who owned the ground north of the loch, now partly gardens and partly Princes Street. It appeared that Hepburn and another person had been casting redd or refuse into the loch, "which is in place of a wall and fence to the good town," and by this means had extended their grounds 5 or 6 ells within the loch and built up three dykes crossing the way to the West Kirk, thereby obstructing the riding of the town's marches and closing up a pleasant and useful walk. Little satisfaction was got from Hepburn, and in February 1705 there occurs a Minute in which the Council recommends the baron bailie of Broughton to convene Robert Hepburn of Bearford before his court in order to prevent his casting redd into the North Loch.

In June 1711 the Minutes make reference to the

settlement of a litigation with Hepburn and a feu given to him of a moor and bog adjoining the North Loch for a feu-duty of £4 Scots. This moor or bog lay at the head of the North Loch and was bounded on the west by an acre of grass belonging to the town called the "Loadman's Aiker," and on the north by the lands of Lochbank. The Agreement also gave Hepburn the right of watering his bestial on the north side of the loch, while reserving to the town the privilege of feeding their swans upon Hepburn's side of the loch. The bounds were marked by march stones.

In 1716 the town purchased Lochbank from Hepburn, and in November 1720 a Minute occurs giving instructions to the Lord Provost, then in London, as follows:—"The good town being now possessed of the estate of Lochbank and the north loch being rather a nuisance than a convenience to the city, the draining of the loch and opening an easy communication with that estate will not only improve and add to the estate but by affording convenient dwellings to a number of persons of note and character and their residences which now are at some distance from the city will be fixt to it. Wherefore we judge it will tend much to the benefit of the community if your Lordship can obtain a clause in an Act of Parliament whereby the execution of so good a design may be encouraged and facilitate." The lands of Lochbank cost the town 39,000 merks Scots money and extended to rather more than 30 acres and included a part of the Kirklands of St Cuthbert's. By this purchase the town became proprietor of the ground lying between the North Loch and the line of Rose Street, including Princes Street.

In the Minutes of the Town Council for 19th March 1740, there is a reference to the North Loch which states that it was the the North Loch. only fence to the city on the north side, and of late had been so drained that encroachments had been made on its area and great prejudice had arisen to His Majesty's Customs and Excise and to the revenue of the city by the ready access through the loch, which allowed smugglers to import everything into the city free from payment of imposts and customs. Wherefore an order was made to stop up the loch till the water reached the ancient boundaries. It seems plain from this and other Minutes to the same effect that before the middle of the eighteenth century the loch was maintained, not for defence and not for amenity, but mainly for the purpose of keeping out smugglers. For about a century before this time Edinburgh had been noted as a place for smuggling. Contraband goods coming from over the seas were landed at the Figgate Burn, or the Drum Sands, or some other convenient place on the coast, and were thence conveyed to the banks of the North Loch and secretly passed through Lady Stair's, or Baxter's, or the Advocate's Close, to cellars or other places of concealment. It is said that there were several underground passages which ran from boathouses on the banks of the loch into the centre of the town. The Union of the Parliaments introduced new taxes, and an army of Customs officers was imported from England, who were far from popular with the sturdy burgesses of Edinburgh. The state of public feeling was shown in the Porteous Riots, and Sir Walter Scott makes one of his characters in the *Heart of Midlothian* (Plumdamus) explain about the North Loch that it enabled "an honest man to fetch sae muckle as a bit anker o' brandy frae Leith to the Lawnmarket, without being rubbit o' the very gudes he'd bought and paid for by a host o' idle English gaugers." At an earlier age the Town Council had brought trouble on themselves because the loch had overflowed its proper bounds, but by this time the difficulty was to keep the water in the loch and to prevent the encroachments of the citizens upon its diminished area. Maitland tells us in his history that in the year 1743 the sluice at the eastern end of the loch was opened to let out the water when the loch became dry. He adds that by the soil of the town incessantly running into it, the loch was about half filled up in 1753 and that probably in less than a century it would be quite levelled.

The building of the North Bridge in 1763 marked the real beginning of the end of the North Loch for the simple reason that it was desirable to build

THE CASTLE BOUNDARIES

24

the piers of the bridge on dry land. A Town Council Minute of 15th February 1764 states that the loch was "now in a good measure drained" and that it was probable that the ground thereby gained would be of great value in due time. Because daily encroachments were being made on the south side, an inquiry was ordered to be made to have the marches cleared up, and it was arranged that the bottom of the loch should be exposed to public roup for cutting grass during the summer. The Committee reported in April following that it was of importance to have the encroachments removed and the boundaries of the loch ascertained, and it was resolved to bring a process of declarator of the town's rights, which was thereupon done, a proceeding which proved to be most unfortunate for the city, as will be narrated below.

A further stage was reached when the Mound began to be formed in 1781, as the execution of this scheme divided the bed of the loch into two parts and stopped the run of the water from the west to the east. In May 1787 the Town Council ordered the drainage of the loch to be carried on "with all possible dispatch." On 28th April 1790 the Town Council received a plan and report from James Gordon, who proposed to run a culvert 3 feet in diameter from the North Bridge all the way to St Cuthbert's Churchyard in order to carry sewage and spring water, including the flow from the Well-house Tower. The report stated with emphasis that the culvert would take off every drop of water from the north side, and that Mr Gordon would answer for making the whole meadow as dry as Princes Street. This work accordingly was ordered to be carried out as soon as possible.

A reference to Edgar's Map, which is dated 1765, shows the bed of the loch as measuring 1700 feet in length from the foot of Ramsay Lodge to the foot of Halkerston's Wynd, and 400 in breadth at the foot of the Gardens below the Advocate's Close, while from the upper point to the West Church the bed is shown as a bog or marsh. Chambers writes that many in common with himself must remember the time when the remains of this sheet of water, consisting of a few pools, served as sliding and skating ground in winter, while the neglected precincts formed an arena for the quarrels between the cowlies of the old and the new town, and in his day woodcock, snipe and waterduck were attracted to what is now the West Gardens by the damp of the locality. The site of the loch in 1790 is described as disgusting below as well as above the bridge. The statute for the improvement of the valley west of the Mound was not passed until 1816, and Lord Cockburn described it as being then an impassable fetid marsh, "open on all sides, the receptacle of many sewers and seemingly of all the worried cats, drowned dogs and blackguardism of the city. Its abomination made it so solitary that the volunteers used to practise ball-firing across it. The men stood on its north side and the targets were set up along the lower edge of the Castle Hill or rock. The only difficulty was in getting across the swamp to place and examine the targets, which could only be done in very dry weather and at one or two places."

The East Gardens, extending to $8\frac{1}{2}$ acres, in like manner remained as a reedy, marshy hollow for long years after the loch had passed away. This area on its eastern side was bounded by what was called the Little Mound, a roadway in line with St Andrew Street, to the east of the present Waverley Bridge; it was effectively drained about the year 1821, and then was let as a nursery. The maps of 100 years ago show in the area between the Waverley Bridge and the North Bridge a street called Canal Street, the name being an allusion to the sheet of water intended to be provided there. In the map given in Hugo Arnot's *History*, published in 1788, the valley from the North Bridge to St Cuthbert's glebe is shown as occupied all the way by a broad canal lying between straight parallel lines. At the eastern end the vegetable market occupied a site under the North Bridge; at the south end of the Little Mound there was a slaughter-house, but both places were at a later date absorbed in the Waverley Station. In the year 1783 the Hallow Fair was held in Bearford's Parks.

While the East Gardens were converted into a nursery, the West Gardens formed the subject of

The North Loch

an Act of Parliament in 1816, under which the proprietors in Princes Street, west of Hanover Street, received authority to enclose and improve the North Loch and the ground on the south side of Princes Street. The West Gardens, therefore, became private property, just as to-day the gardens lying between Queen Street and Heriot Row are private property. But, before dealing with this chapter, it may be proper to refer to one or two other matters of history, beginning with some of the litigations of which the Gardens have been the innocent cause.

CHAPTER II

WHEN the new town was being projected the necessity arose of obtaining an extension of the royalty so that the new area might be within the jurisdiction of the Town Council. The first efforts in this direction were unsuccessful, but the Magistrates were supported by a large body of influential gentlemen throughout Scotland, and in 1767 an Act was passed to extend the royalty over the fields on the north side of the city, and "to enlarge and beautify the town by opening new streets to the north and south, removing the markets and shambles and turning the North Loch into a canal with walks and terraces on each side." Advertisements were at the same time published by the Magistrates desiring plans to be given in conform to which buildings might be erected in the most regular, handsome and commodious manner. Plans were lodged accordingly; the design by James Craig was approved and adopted, and a gold medal was awarded to the successful architect.

This contemplated the erection of a long row of dwelling-houses on the north side of Princes Street; on the south side, to the west of the North Bridge, the sloping ground was shown free of buildings, and as laid out for pleasure ground with a canal in the valley. The Town Council, however, following the usual practice, reserved right to depart from the design, and in their feuing conditions they provided that if houses came to be built on the south side they should not be nearer to the houses on the north side than 96 feet. The ground now occupied by the Railway Hotel was in fact feued for building to certain parties who in 1770 petitioned the Town Council for a further feuing area on a frontage extending 110 feet west of the present Waverley Steps, the purpose being to erect workshops thereon. To this request the Town Council agreed, making the condition, however, that no building erected on this area should rise higher than the level of Princes Street. This proposal led to protests and objections on the part of the other feuars in the street. They alleged that their genteel houses had been built in reliance on the general plan ; that the Town Council were breaking faith in allowing mean and irregular buildings to be put on ground designed as an open space ; and that the beauty of the whole area was about to be ruined. An extraordinary outcry arose, and in 1771 the feuars brought an action of declarator and damages against the Town Council and at the same time presented a Bill of Suspension and Interdict. This Bill was refused by the Court of Session, but the House of Lords reversed the decision and ordered the Court of Session to pass the Bill and conjoin it with the Action of Declarator. The judgment of the House of Lords was delivered by Lord Mansfield and has often been referred to as proving that bad law and good sense may go together very well.

"Can your Lordships approve the conduct of this Corporation on the contemptible idea upon which this conduct has been endeavoured to be justified? . . . In this matter, my Lords, I consider the Corporation of Edinburgh merely as a Committee of city lands, but I would have the Corporation remember that their character is different. If a mere Committee for enriching this Corporation, what title had they to a national contribution, what the purpose of calling to their assistance noblemen of the first rank in the nation, of advising with people of distinction and taste? No, my Lords, these things speak the gentlemen's meaning at the time. Of a sudden, however, forgetful of their character, they sink into a burgh committee, profit is the word, the elegance of the plan is thrown away, Canal Street appears. I should be glad to know whether the gentlemen of taste I have mentioned, My Lords Alemore and Kames, Mr Commissioner Clerk and Mr Adams were consulted about these new erections which I am told vie in deformity with those of the old town. I could say a great deal more upon this subject, but I do not choose and I hope we shall hear no more of the matter."

This judgment, however, was not given on the

merits of the case, but merely at an incidental stage. The case proceeded in the Court of Session, where finally a decision was given in favour of the Town Council, which again was appealed. The Town Council might have had a difficult journey in the House of Lords, but by this time the buildings in question were almost completed and a compromise was seen to be desirable. Accordingly the parties agreed upon a submission to Mr David Rae, a well-known advocate, who afterwards became Lord Justice Clerk. In 1776 he pronounced his decree arbitral. It provided that the buildings on the south side of Princes Street were to be restricted to the area between the Bridge and the present Waverley Steps; that within the feu to the west thereof workshops might be erected below the level of Princes Street; that farther west, almost as far as Hanover Street, the ground was to be occupied in perpetuity as a pleasure ground; that westwards from this point the Town Council were to have full power to feu ground for building, provided that the space between the building lines was not less than 96 feet. The subject is dealt with at length in Book I. of the Old Edinburgh Club.

Lord Mansfield's decision marks a stage in the history of the Princes Street Gardens. The citizens **The Building** realised the importance of the issue **Prohibitions.** that had been raised, and some years later the Gardens were safeguarded by a number of Acts of Parliament. The first of

The Old Town from Princes Street (West)

those is dated in 1816 and regulated the erection of buildings on the Mound and prohibited buildings on the south side of Princes Street west of the Mound, with the exception of St John's Episcopal Church. In 1827 a further Act prohibited the erection of buildings in the East Gardens, excepting a public theatre or playhouse, the prohibition being, however, limited to a period of twenty - one years. The prohibition was made perpetual by an Act passed in 1831 and was declared to be enforceable by any proprietor or householder in the city. In 1841 the Act was passed, which authorised the erection of the Scott Monument, and again the prohibitions were confirmed and the exception in favour of the theatre was repealed.

The first-mentioned of these Acts dated in 1816 was an Improvement Act, and authorised the conversion into gardens of the ground west of the Mound. Certain powers were granted to improve and enclose the area lying between Princes Street and the line which separated the ancient from the extended royalty. This line ran from the keystone of the middle arch of the North Bridge westwards to the north side of the Castle, along the middle of the low ground formerly the North Loch. The exact line came to be of importance in a litigation with the War Department, which will be referred to below. The 1816 Act also contained a clause in favour of the proprietors of Princes Street between

Hanover Street and Hope Street, authorising them to contract and agree with the Town Council or other persons for leases or feus of the area " for the purpose of laying out the same in whole or in part in a garden, nursery for trees, or pleasure ground, or under grass, or otherwise embellishing or enclosing the same." Accordingly these proprietors, in order to put themselves into a proper position to deal with the West Gardens as a whole, obtained the following rights : (a) a lease from the Town Council for the period of ninety-nine years of the area belonging to the community, extending to about 29 acres; (b) a lease of a similar duration of portions of the Ramsay Garden property then belonging to General Ramsay ; (c) an agreement with the Crown for the occupation of the north bank, extending to 2058 square yards, and also of the west and south banks of the Castle, extending to 609 square yards. Under this last agreement the occupation was to endure until the lands were wanted for the public service. By these means the proprietors became possessed of the West Gardens, which they continued to administer until the year 1876 when their rights were taken over by the Corporation. This chapter of the history is deserving of more than a passing reference, but meantime mention falls to be made of some litigations concerning the area.

When the first experiments were being made for draining the North Loch part of the area was of course converted into dry land and questions arose

as to marches and boundaries. The North Loch
and also the banks and braes of the Castle were
claimed in property by the town
under a Charter granted by King
James VI. in the year 1603, one
of the Golden Charters which that King was in
the habit of granting. This title expressly gave to
the Corporation the North Loch, lands, pools and
marches thereof, and the south and north banks and
braes on both sides of the Castle and that part of
the burgh called Under the Castlehill towards the
north to the head of the bank and from thence by the
north and so down to the North Loch. For a long
period prior to 1603 the town had been in possession
of the North Loch, and the inhabitants had enjoyed
the right of perambulating and drying clothes upon,
and otherwise using the north and south banks of
the Castle, which were then open and unenclosed.
As certain parties began to occupy pieces of ground
in and near the North Loch or on the margin thereof,
the Corporation brought an action to define the
bounds of their property. In this action they called
as parties the Governor of the Castle and the Officers
of State for the interests of the Crown ; and among
others, the proprietor of what is now Ramsay Garden,
whose property extended from the Castlehill down
to the North Loch ; and a Mr Tod, whose property
adjoined Ramsay Lodge on the east side and who
had certain tan pits at the margin of the loch. An
appearance was made for the Earl of Loudon, then

*The Action of
Declarator in
1769.*

Governor of the Castle, and certain of the defenders, and an order for production of titles was made by the Court. The bearing and significance of the action does not seem to have been appreciated by the defenders who failed to obey the orders of the Court, and after various stages had been gone through the Court granted a decree in the town's favour in the year 1771. This decree was allowed to become final and was duly extracted. It was, however, a barren victory, which led the Corporation into much trouble and expense, as later on it was found to be ineffective against the Ramsay Lodge proprietors, and was also reduced in 1801 by the proprietors of Tod's property, and again in 1862 by the Crown. While it subsisted, the Corporation held, as they believed, a title to the Castle banks, which are described as rising from the public road or Grassmarket on the south and descending to the loch on the north, including also the Esplanade or parade ground in between. The action brought by the Crown in 1862 will be considered shortly, but meantime a reference is necessary to the dispute which arose between Allan Ramsay and the city.

It is well known that Ramsay Lodge has its name from the celebrated author of the *Gentle* *Shepherd*, who built as a sort of Allan Ramsay's Case. town and country house the octagonal villa still partly visible at Ramsay Gardens. Like other properties built on the north side of the ridge, this one had garden ground

descending to the North Loch, and in the old
titles the site was described as bounded by the
North Loch "upon the north pairt thereof." The
Act of the Guild Court may still be perused which
authorised Allan Ramsay to enclose his ground on
the Castle Hill in the year 1750. His ground
marched on the west with the Castle Hill and the
Castle bank, from which it appears to have been
separated by a garden dyke, while another dyke had
also at one time existed on the north boundary.
Allan Ramsay, the poet, died in 1758 and was
succeeded in the property by his son, Allan Ramsay,
the painter. In the year 1776 the Town Council
were digging a drain or canal through the North
Loch and a complaint was made by the artist to
the Sheriff of Edinburgh that this drain in the
direction it was taking would come through and
intersect his back ground to his great hurt and
prejudice. The litigation was perhaps not a very
serious one, but the papers show that it created a
certain amount of excitement at the time. The
Answers called forth Replies; these in turn led to
Duplies, then to Triplies and ultimately to Quadruplies, in which much ancient history is given; and
while the Corporation blamed Allan Ramsay for his
attempt to mar public improvements and the beauty
of the environs of the New Town, the latter stated
that "such declamation truly comes with a bad grace
from the town of Edinburgh after what has been
done to the west of the north end of the bridge,"

this being, of course, a reference to Lord Mansfield's decision. The configuration of the ground has been altered entirely by the railway lines, which were laid on a low level, whereas it rather appears that the loch did not usually come so far south as the railway, since Ramsay's ground extended across the railway and a little to the north thereof. Ramsay pleaded that the canal was being diverted so as to encroach on his property, whereas his property would have been avoided and the canal kept in the middle of the valley if it had been continued in a straight line from the middle arch of the bridge where it set out. Edgar's Plan (1742) indicates that no part either of the North Loch or of the bog or marsh at the head thereof extended farther south than the line of the north boundary of Ramsay's property. In the Crown case to be mentioned immediately, this point was greatly stressed as the Corporation claimed about 150 feet of ground south of this line.

An Interim Interdict was granted, upon which a litigation ensued in the course of which long pleadings were lodged by both parties. The Magistrates produced and founded on their decree in the Declarator case mentioned above, but no effect was given to this plea. On the contrary, the Interim Interdict (11th September 1776) stood unrecalled and Ramsay continued to possess his whole grounds without further molestation.

The next litigation to be mentioned seems almost

The Railway

to be a connecting-link between the past and the
present, since on the one hand it takes us back to

the Declarator of 1771 and is concerned with the old subject of the
bounds or marches of the North Loch,
and on the other hand the immediate cause was
the first construction of the railway lines which
now intersect the Gardens. It was in or about the
year 1844 that the Edinburgh and Glasgow Railway
Company took possession of a portion of the valley
which formerly had been the site of the North Loch
or the marshes adjacent thereto. Before the Railway
Company had obtained their Act of Parliament the
Corporation had agreed to convey to them the
ground required for their works, and the price to be
paid was referred to certain arbiters and was not
settled until long after the railway had been formed.
This litigation was a *cause célèbre* in its day and
must have been popular with the legal profession,
which managed to keep it going from the year 1849
to the year 1862. Voluminous papers, including
several prints containing over 200 pages and a
collection of maps and plans, bear testimony to the
capacity of former agents and officials for taking
pains which nowadays we may think were worthy
of a better cause.

The case began in 1849 in the form of a Declarator
by the principal officers of Her Majesty's Ordnance
against the Corporation, the individual members being
cited by name. The Lord Provost was Sir William

Princes Street Gardens

Johnstone of Kirkhill, and with him there were four
Bailies, the Dean of Guild, the Treasurer, the
Convener of Trades and twenty-five Councillors.
The pursuers claimed that their property of the
Castle and Castle Hill of Edinburgh extended to the
line of a certain old wall or dyke in the valley, which
ran east and west at a distance of some 146 feet
north of the Wellhouse Tower, and they craved
the Court to ordain parties to concur in placing
march stones along the line of this wall or dyke, and
in this way to mark off the property of the Castle
from the property of the town. This old wall or
dyke was not then in existence, but it had formed a
continuation of the north boundary of the Ramsay
Lodge property which has been referred to above,
and it ran thence until it reached St Cuthbert's
glebe, where it joined a cross wall forming the
eastern boundary of the glebe. The wall had been
taken down when the Princes Street proprietors got
possession of the Gardens in 1818, but numerous
witnesses still survived, who were able to describe
its location, which proved to be on the north side of
the present railway lines. This involved, of course,
that the railway had been constructed on Crown
property and not on town property, and so the
agreement between the Corporation and the Railway
Company was at stake, and with it the compensation
to be paid for the ground appropriated by the Railway
Company. The plea of the Corporation was that the
North Loch extended to the foot of the Castle bank

The Old Town from Princes Street (East)

and Castle rocks, and that under the Charter of 1603 not only the North Loch but also the banks and braes of the Castle had been granted to the town.

The Corporation also pleaded that the subject was *res judicata* under the decree obtained by them in 1771 in the declaratory action dealt with above. It has been mentioned that this decree had an unfortunate history, and rather unwisely the Corporation made claims under it, which now appear to have been extravagant. They claimed, in fact, to own the banks and braes of the Castle from the Grassmarket on the one side to the North Loch on the other, including the Esplanade or parade ground ; that is, everything not contained within the actual walls of the Castle itself.

In the course of the proceedings a proof was allowed and a diligence granted for recovery of documents upon which a strange event happened. The Town Clerk was Mr James Lawrie, and when he appeared as a witness he produced a Charter to the town granted by King Charles I. in the year 1636, which displaced the earlier Charter of King James VI. and therefore affected the validity of the decree of 1771 which had proceeded upon the earlier Charter. There is a passage in Maitland's history which refers to the Charter of 1603 and states as follows :—" Divers articles in the above charter being judged derogatory to the honour and dignity of the Crown the Edinburghers voluntarily offered to resign the same to King Charles I., and in

lieu thereof entreated him to grant them a Charter
to confirm all their rights, privileges and immunities
which was accordingly done in the year 1636."
Maitland gives a translation of King Charles's
Charter, which narrates the doubts which had arisen
regarding the previous grant of 1603, the renunciation by the City and the petition for a new Charter.
The deed then proceeds to ratify various grants in
favour of the City, but does not include the grant
of 1603, and in the enumeration of the subjects
conveyed there is no mention of the Castle, Castle
banks, or grounds adjoining thereto, but merely of
"the lake of our said city called the North Loch,
soil, land, marches and myres of the same." The
Charter narrates at length the renunciation which
had been made of the Castle banks.

In this altered position the Corporation put
forward the courageous plea that the Charter of
1636 had virtually been reduced by the decree of
1771, which while it stood determined the rights of
parties. To meet the new circumstances the Crown
deemed it expedient to bring another action against
the Corporation for reduction of this decree and for
declarator of its rights.

This second action was initiated in 1853 when
Duncan M'Laren was Lord Provost. It craved the
Court to find and declare that the decree of 1771
was of no avail, force, strength or effect, and that
the property of the Castle included not only the
north bank and a track of level ground at the foot

thereof, but also the west bank and the south bank, as also the Esplanade or parade ground. The subjects referred to formed a detached portion of the Parish of Canongate, which seems an odd fact. This no doubt gives the reason why the soldiers who died in the Castle were buried in the Canongate Churchyard. The visitor to this burial-ground cannot fail to notice the tall obelisk of red granite surmounted by a cross which occupies the centre of the low ground. It bears the inscription, " In memory of the soldiers who died in Edinburgh Castle situated in the parish of Canongate interred here with military honours from the year 1682 to 1880."

The two processes came before Lord Neaves, and after being conjoined they pursued a leisurely course and the facts were inquired into in great detail. The Lord Ordinary gave a decision against the town, and in 1859 his decision was confirmed by the First Division, whereupon the processes were carried to the House of Lords. In the decree of the Court of Session the only right reserved to the Corporation was in respect of the roadway of Johnston Terrace formed in the year 1828. Leave to form this road had been obtained from the Duke of Wellington when Master-General of the Ordnance, and in respect of this invasion of the rights at that time held by the Princes Street proprietors, a payment of £315 had been made by the Corporation.

The case which the Corporation presented to the House of Lords was prepared by Andrew Rutherford

Clark, afterwards Lord Rutherford Clark. The claim formerly made to the banks and braes of the Castle was now abandoned and the appeal was confined to the minor question concerning the bounds of the North Loch. The Corporation contended that only the Castle banks had been renounced, that under their titles they were proprietors of the North Loch and its mires and marshes, and that these included the whole level ground at the foot of the Castle banks and at least the whole ground lying to the northward of the old city wall.

The case for the War Department was prepared by Mr Moncrieff and Mr Gifford, afterwards Lord Justice Clerk Moncrieff and Lord Gifford. It contained some rather scathing remarks about the Corporation, for example, that their claims had been of the most startling and alarming description; that the Charter of 1636 had been withheld and concealed by them; that they no longer pushed their claims to the very base of the ramparts of the Castle, or pretended right to the Esplanade where troops had been drilled and exercised for centuries; "but at the end of this long, expensive and anxious litigation the appellants have found themselves compelled to admit that the great bulk of their claims were absolutely groundless, and their whole demand is now restricted to the comparatively unimportant question of the right of property in a strip of level ground 50 yards broad and little more than 300 yards long; and it would appear that the sole or almost the

sole object of the appellants is to enable them to
retain the compensation money paid by the Edinburgh and Glasgow Railway Company for the right
of passage through this ground."

The title of the War Department to the Castle
of Edinburgh was traced back to the Scots Act of
Parliament of 1455, Cap. 41, by which it was annexed
to the Crown and declared to be incapable of being
alienated or made the subject of a Royal grant. This
of itself would have sufficed to displace the Charter
of 1603 and partly explained its renunciation by
the Corporation. The validity and effect of the
decree of 1771 was also criticised and a detailed
argument was presented upon the evidence of
witnesses and of authentic writings and plans.
Emphasis was laid upon the line of the old wall
forming the north boundary of Allan Ramsay's
property, upon the boundary between the ancient
and the extended royalty, and upon the circumstance
that the ground in question had always been held
as part of the Parish of Canongate, and been assessed
for poor rates and other burdens accordingly.

The House of Lords decided the appeal in
favour of the Crown on 4th March 1862, and the
case is reported in 24 Dunlop. March stones were
accordingly placed on the boundary line where
they may still be seen. The boundary runs along
Ramsay Garden, down into the valley and across the
railway near to the east footbridge, on the north side
of which a square granite stone marked No. VI has

been placed ; thence roughly it runs along the low shrubbery on the north side of the railway almost to the west footbridge, before reaching which it crosses the railway and runs to a point on the footway west of this footbridge where a march stone marked No. I has been placed. The papers do not disclose the manner in which the compensation money paid by the railway was allocated, except that the Corporation were paid for their part at the rate of a few shillings per square yard. For the land in the East Gardens the Corporation received £2566, 7s. for 10,346 square yards, being at the rate of 4s. 11½d. per square yard.

The mention of this case brings the narrative down almost to the present day, and many people **The Railway Arbitration, 1892.** still young will remember when the railway lines in the Gardens were duplicated. Long before this date the Princes Street proprietors had gone out of existence, and the Corporation was in possession of the Gardens, as they had been in possession of the North Loch in a former age. These proprietors were brought into being by the City Act of 1816, and their rights were taken over by the Corporation under the Improvement Act of 1876, after an existence of some sixty years. They had possessed the West Gardens, including the Castle banks round to Johnston Terrace, and in laying out the grounds they had been advised by James Skene of Rubislaw, who was related to George Drummond, the famous

Lord Provost of the City. Mention has been made
of certain rights obtained by the proprietors, including
a lease of part of the Ramsay Lodge property. This
area was bought up by the Corporation in 1876 from
James Lamond, the successor of Allan Ramsay.
The Castle banks continue to be occupied under
the Agreement made by the proprietors in 1818,
and the title to this portion of the Gardens is
regarded as equivalent to a perpetual right for the
reason that part of the area has been appropriated
by the Railway Company, and the Crown is not
now in a position to utilise the subjects for the
public service.

There still remain two portions of the West
Gardens not included in the rights of the proprietors
mentioned above. One of these is an area at the
Mound extending to about 447 square yards,
belonging to the Trustees who are the owners of
the National Gallery on the Mound, through the
greater part of which the railway runs in the tunnel.
The Corporation have no title to this area, which,
however, has been handed over to them and now
forms part of the Gardens. The other portion is
at the west end, being a portion of the glebe of
St Cuthbert's, mentioned in an earlier part of this
narrative. The Princes Street proprietors obtained
a Feu Charter of this area from the West Church
ministers in 1831, in which the ground is described
as lying to the east of the present east wall of the
churchyard and consisting of one acre and five falls

Scots measure. From the plan it appears that the north boundary of this area is in line with the north wall of the churchyard, which line it continues eastwards for some 210 feet or thereby ; thence the boundary runs south in a straight line till it crosses the railway just west of the west footbridge, touching the property of the Crown at or near to the march stone marked No. I. The north wall of the churchyard is about 280 feet south of Princes Street. The Feu Charter bears to be granted subject to the restrictions imposed by the Act 3 George IV. c. 27 (1822), which prohibits the Ministers, Sir Henry Moncrieff Wellwood and David Dickson, from granting a feu for building of "any part of the said glebe lands lying to the east of the churchyard of St Cuthbert's or to the east of the road leading from the south gate of the said churchyard situated between the two manses towards the Grassmarket." This area, therefore, is subject to a prohibition against building in much the same way as the areas affected by the City Act of 1816.

The Railway Arbitration of 1892 followed upon an Act, obtained in the preceding year by the North British Railway, and related to the West and East Gardens, both of which were then being administered by the Corporation. Parties having failed to reach an agreement as to the compensation to be paid, arbiters were appointed by the parties, and when they had differed in their opinions the submission devolved upon the oversman, Lord Shand. The claim of the Corporation was stated roundly at £150,000, but the amount awarded was a more modest sum, namely £26,500, made up as follows:— (1) £23,500 for the lands belonging to the Corporation; (2) £2000 for their interest in the Crown Lands; and (3) £1000 for their interest in the Bank of Scotland's lands in the East Gardens. It came out in the course of the proceedings that in 1873 the Railway Company had applied for a strip of ground on the north side of their lines in the East Gardens, extending to 1007 square yards, and that this had been voluntarily conveyed to them by the Corporation for the sum of £2000, being at a rate rather less than £2 per square yard. This incident proved to be a serious obstacle in the proceedings of 1892, as Lord Shand attached importance to it as a precedent. The details of the case need not be elaborated, but two points were safeguarded: one, that the lines in the East Gardens were to be used as an access only and not to be used for station purposes; and the other, that the lines were to be embanked and planted so as to screen the railway. These matters are provided for in the 1891 Act.

The Award makes reference to the Bank of Scotland property in the East Gardens. These gardens were never controlled by the proprietors of houses in Princes Street, but had been let in 1832 to Thomas Cleghorn, a seedsman and florist. In the tack they are described as "All and Whole the eastmost division of the North Loch lying

between the Great Earthen Mound and the Little
Earthen Mound." The duration was four periods
of seven years each from 1832, and the subjects
were to be utilised as a nursery ground. There was
a provision in favour of the tenant that he "should
have liberty to admit any persons of respectability
to the privilege of walking within the said enclosed
area for payment of such a sum as he might think
proper not exceeding 10s. 6d. a year for each key
given out for that purpose." The Directors and
officers of the Bank of Scotland were to have access
to the whole of the ground and to be furnished with
keys free of charge; and the rent to be paid was
£30 yearly. Grant in his history states that these
gardens were first laid out in 1830, and, after suffering
mutilation by the Edinburgh and Glasgow Railway,
they were re-formed and ornamented anew in 1849-50
at an expense of about £4500.

The property of the Bank of Scotland resembled
the Ramsay Lodge property in respect that it had
originally descended to the shores of the North Loch.
The Bank's property extends into the valley in the
East Gardens, but does not go across the railway.
On the west it comes close to the steps leading to
the stairway which ascends to the Mound, and on
the east it does not reach as far as the Waverley
Bridge, the ground for over 100 feet from that street
being the property of the town.

The property of the Bank consists of two parts.
The westmost or the larger part is held under

The Bank of Scotland

a restriction against building and an obligation to maintain it as garden ground, and it pays £1, 1s. per annum to the city. The east portion is held by the Bank free from restriction. For many years the Corporation have been lessees of the Bank's land at the nominal rent of £1, 1s. per annum, which forms a cross-entry with the ground rent beforementioned in the City Accounts. The Corporation also bear the expense of maintaining the ground as a garden. The last lease from the Bank expired at Martinmas 1911, so that the Corporation now hold the Bank's lands as yearly tenants.

CHAPTER III

THE FREEDOM OF THE CITY

IN order to understand the conditions of burghal life in former times, it is necessary to have some knowledge of the early conception of citizenship. As is well known, the freedom of the burgh was not the possession of all the inhabitants, but was restricted to the class known as burgesses. The Corporation of the burgh did not consist of the whole people, but only of burgesses or freemen, and these only were entitled to enjoy the privileges of the burgh and to participate in its government. The burgh was essentially a community of freemen, known as free burgesses, neighbours, good men, *probi seu boni homines.* Freedom in this sense did not, of course, refer to personal liberty, as we now use the term, but to the enjoyment of the rights of citizenship as then understood.

The main condition of freedom in the early times of burghs appears to have been the possession of heritable property. The Laws of the Burghs provided that no man might be a King's burgess unless he did the service appropriate to "ane rude of land at the least"; that every burgess should give to the King five pence yearly for each rood of land that he defended; and that any man who acquired a "borowage" and dwelt therein for a year and a day without challenge should be "evirmare free as a burges wythin that kyng's burgh." At an early stage the burghal communities assumed the power to regulate the grant of freedom; and burgesses were admitted by the Magistrates with the consent of the community, subject to conditions which varied from time to time. Generally these conditions provided that applicants should settle and remain within the burgh; and should swear fealty to the King, the bailies and the community; and should pay as the price of burgess-ship a sum of money towards the common funds.

Every burgess became subject to various duties and obligations. He had to defend his burrowage; and to have "stob and staik" there, that is to build and maintain a house upon his land. He had also to attend the head courts of the burgh; to take his part in watching and warding; to pay his proportion of stents and common civic burdens; and to sustain in turn such offices as the law imposed on freemen. These various obligations were known in Scotland, and also in England, by the term "scot and lot."

On the other hand, burgess-ship conferred important privileges. Commerce was forbidden by law to any class except burgesses, who were free to buy and sell throughout Scotland. Foreign merchants could only buy within burgh and from a burgess, and were prohibited from selling elsewhere than in burgh or to others than burgesses. All suits and actions arising within a burgh were heard and decided in the Burgh Court with the exception of pleas pertaining to the Crown, and a burgess might decline the jurisdiction of any other court. A burgess could dispose as he pleased of all lands within burgh purchased by him, and might sell property acquired by inheritance subject to certain conditions, particularly the complex conditions which regulated the rights of succession. The burgesses were, however, free from many of the exactions for which vassals were liable under the feudal tenure.

The burgesses possessed the right of electing the Magistrates of the burgh. The old laws provided that the alderman and bailies should be chosen by "the gude men of the toune, lele and of guid fame"; and at the sight and by the consideration of the "whole community." These expressions have been made the subject of controversy, but it is now generally understood that they mean one and the same thing, namely, the free inhabitants of the burgh, duly admitted as burgesses, who performed the duties and possessed the privileges incident to that estate.

While the inhabitants of the burgh were divided into two classes, being either free or unfree, the **The Merchant Guild.** former class was subject to further division *inter se* by means of various organisations which, though subordinate, were of great influence. The most ancient as well as the most important of these was the Guild of

The Merchant Guild

Merchants. As the name indicates, this guild was primarily an association for trading purposes, but at one stage of its history it was something more, since in Edinburgh and elsewhere it attained a position which enabled it to overshadow and apparently to absorb the municipal organisation. In the absence of documents, its early history is largely a subject of conjecture upon which a variety of theories have been constructed, one of these being to the effect that the Merchant Guild was the predecessor of the Town Council; that the Council evolved from the Guild, so that, as it is expressed, the Guild first made the Council. Whether this is right or not, the Guild of Edinburgh undoubtedly had its origin in remote times.

One of the laws of William the Lion (1164-1214) allowed the merchants of the realm to have their Merchant Guild or *gilda mercatoria*, and conferred on merchants a monopoly in the trade of certain commodities. About the year 1249 the Statutes of the Guild were compiled, and these deal not only with trade but also with subjects of general concern to burghs. These Statutes provided that no one should be received into the guild for a less payment than 40s., excepting the sons and daughters of burgesses and guild brethren. The members were bound to participate in common religious ceremonies; to provide for sick and decayed brethren; to live together in peace and concord; and to be fair and honest in their trading relations. But other Statutes deal with the general administration of the burgh and seem to indicate that the guild and the burgh were to a large extent indistinguishable.

The published Records of the City begin with a Minute dated in 1403 : "The first Head Guild held after the feast of Saint Michael in the Tolbuith of the burgh of Edinburgh, the brethren of the Gild being called and compearing ; 3rd October 1403— The officers of the Gild are elected as follows :— Provost Alexander Naper ; Dean of Guild and Keeper of the Kirk Wark, Symon de Schele ; Bailie of Leith, John Robertson." In this Minute the date 1403 has been erroneously transcribed for 1453. Its terms indicate that the Town Council represented, and were an elective committee of the Merchant Guild.

In explanation it has been stated that the guild brethren were the patricians of the burgh owing to their wealth and influence, and were thus enabled to monopolise the functions of the Town Council. Marwick, however, suggests that the Merchant Guild may have been under the jurisdiction of the Town Council and regulated by them in the same way as the burgh ; or that the Merchant Guild may then have included the members of all the other guilds of the burgh, and in this way have become co-extensive with and equivalent to the community of burgesses.

The relation of the Merchant Guild to the general body of burgesses is difficult to trace. In

A View of the Cross of Edinburgh from the West This ancient Fabric was taken down 13 of March 1756

THE MERCAT CROSS

the burgh the existence of merchants presupposes the existence of artisans and craftsmen. That all guild brethren were burgesses seems certain, but that all burgesses were entitled to enter the guild is uncertain. Be that as it may, it happened in process of time that the distinction between the merchants and the crafts became broader and more marked. The mercantile classes became wealthier and more important, and the crafts became identified with the poorer classes. Then the Merchant Guild made the practice of certain trades a ground of exclusion. Thus it became a disqualification for a man to hawk his wares on the street or to work with his own hands. In turn the craftsmen formed organisations for their own defence following the model of the Merchant Guild, and they asserted a right to share in the government of the burgh. In some such way there originated a strife between the merchants and crafts in Edinburgh which formed a feature of municipal life for several centuries.

In 1469 the ancient right of the burgesses to elect the officers of the burgh was arbitrarily taken away by an Act of Parliament, which provided that the retiring Council should choose their successors, the new Council ; and that the old and new Councils acting together should choose the aldermen, bailies, dean of guild and other officers of the burgh. The Act also provided that one person from each of the Trade Incorporations should vote along with the old and new Councils in these annual elections of officers. This Act inaugurated the system of close and secret administration which endured so long as a blot upon the municipal history of Scotland. Its bearing upon the Merchant Guild was not less momentous since in terms it deprived the merchants of any exclusive right they had possessed in electing the members and office-bearers of the Town Council; granted some recognition to the claims of the craftsmen; and gave a new status to the Dean of Guild, which was independent of the members of the guild. From this date onwards the Dean of Guild falls to be regarded, not as head of the Guild, but as an officer of the Corporation, and he was elected, not by the members of the guild, but in the same way as the Provost and Bailies.

From this time, therefore, it seems plain that the Merchant Guild must have lost something of its former importance. It seems that it became a department of the Town Council and that its funds were alienated to the common uses of the burgh. From certain Minutes of the Town Council in 1500-1 it is inferred that the Town Council also supervised the ordinary affairs of the guild. In 1503 an Act of Parliament provided that no burgesses or guild brethren should be created without the consent of the Town Council, and that the profit of making guild brethren should go to the common good of the burgh and be expended on the common work. The Merchant Guild ceased to exist in the proper sense of the term, and was transformed into the

Guildry, over which the Magistrates exercised authority so that its members were essentially subject to their control.

In this state of matters the merchants still experienced the necessity for a corporate life in order to raise funds for charitable purposes, to protect their trading interests, and to exclude and punish outsiders. Therefore they approached the Town Council with a request for a Charter or Seal of Cause. In 1518 this was granted to them on the supplication "of the haill merchandis and gild brether of this burgh"; and in this manner they acquired anew the rights and privileges for which the Merchant Guild had originally come into existence. The Seal of Cause granted them the altar and aisle of the Holy Blood in St Giles' Church; gave them power to elect a Master of Faculty and other officers; to hold courts and punish transgressors; and to attend to the freighting of ships lading at Leith.

Nothwithstanding the developments mentioned above, the merchants continued to have a majority of representatives on the Town Council, and also a monopoly in using merchandise. On these two points the struggle between merchants and crafts-men continued for more than a century, the latter claiming to have a larger representation on the Town Council and also right to become guild brethren and engage in merchandise. An Act of 1466 had excluded craftsmen from the guild and had enacted that no craftsmen should use merchandise unless he renounced his craft. In 1500 the Court of the Four Burghs ordained that no craftsman should use merchandise in burgh but only use his own craft. Both of the claims put forward by the craftsmen were worth fighting for, and, while emphasis is commonly laid on the claim for greater representation on the Town Council, it is possible that the merchants were even more concerned to maintain their trading monopoly. For this purpose it was important to them that the Dean of Guild, who had an extensive jurisdiction and was regarded as the head of the mercantile community, should continue to be "ane merchant trafficquand," and that the officers of the burgh should be merchants, " honest and substantial burgesses."

The struggle developed into something akin to a civic war. In 1544 the craftsmen were roused by an infringement of their liberties at the annual elections, and the deacons drew their swords in the Council Chamber, avowing their determination to defend their rights. They were overpowered and imprisoned but the affair was afterwards compromised. Again, in 1582, there were tumults in the town at the time of the elections, and the craftsmen invaded the Council Chamber and threatened to destroy the Books and Records. These acts of violence and the popular irritation led the Privy Council to interfere, and they required both parties to submit their differences to the arbitration of King James. His decision or decreet-arbitral was issued in the

The Craftsmen's Rights

following year and established the sett of the burgh. It gave the craftsmen eight representatives, out of a council of twenty-five, namely, six deacons and two others. It ordained that the provost, bailies, dean of guild and treasurer, should be in all time coming of the estate and calling of merchants. It also opened the guildry to the craftsmen. "Toward the lang controversie for the gildre it is finally appoyntit . . . that als weill craftsmen as merchants sall be received and admitted gild brether; and the ane not to be refusit nor secludit therefra mair nor the uther; they being burgesses of the burgh als meitt and qualified thairfor; and that gild-brether have liberty to use merchandise." Their admission and trial were to be in the power and hands of the Town Council. The dean of guild was to have a council of six persons, three of them merchants and three craftsmen. If any craftsmen exercising merchandise became a magistrate of the burgh, he should in that case leave his craft and not occupy the same during the time of his office.

Undoubtedly this decree materially raised the status of the craftsmen, although it did not realise altogether the pious wish of the King that both parties should put into oblivion all bypast enmities and live in amity, "as they are of ane city, swa to be of ane mind." Thereafter it was open to the Town Council to admit any burgess as a guild brother and thus to qualify him to use merchandise.

61

The Freedom of the City

This was construed as meaning the exclusive privilege of trading within the burgh, except on market days when unfreemen and outsiders might sell their wares. The guildry continued to be a higher estate than the burgess-ship; but its basis was broadened and it was not thereafter an exclusive body of merchants.

A Minute of the Town Council, of date 6th January 1584-85, enacted that no one should be received guild brother unless he was of honest, discreet and good conversation, "swa tryet and fund be the provost, bailyeis and counsall." The fee to be paid by the eldest son of a burgess was 13s. 4d.; by other sons, 20s.; by apprentices, £10; and all others had to pay a duty of £40. In addition there was a means qualification; he that was of the merchant vocation was to be "esteemit in movebill guids worth ane thousand merks"; the craftsman not using his craft was to be worth the same amount; the handy labourer using his craft was to be worth 500 merks.

To complete this statement a reference should be made to the Merchant Company of the city. Their Charter was obtained in 1681, and again the main purposes were trading and charitable; to provide "effectual means for improving of their trade and preventing all abuses therein . . . that none shall have liberty to exercise the said trade within the said city or privileges thereof until first they enter themselves members of the said Society and pay the entry and dues." The Merchant Company is the modern Merchant Guild, and it is a condition of membership still that every applicant shall become a burgess and guild brother of the city.

It has been stated above that the distinction between the merchants and the craftsmen, or trades, The may not have been strongly marked Incorporations. in the early practice of the burgh, and that all sections of burgesses may originally have been included in the same organisation. The pretensions of the merchants, who have been described as haughty and avaricious, prompted the exclusion of the crafts from the guild; and the oppression under which the latter suffered induced them to combine together for the purpose of self-defence. The movement lasted for a long period and the new combinations encountered a variety of difficulties. Whereas the Government had aided the Merchant Guild and given them protection for their monopolies, the experience of the craftsmen was quite the reverse, and they received little countenance or support by way of Royal Charter or Act of Parliament. An early Act passed in 1424 had empowered the crafts to choose deacons or kirkmasters, who were to be wise men having authority "ower the layff," that is, over the other members. But later Acts denounced the deacons as "rycht dangerous"; and the conventions of craftsmen as leading to violence and "greit troubill." It was a tradition in Edinburgh that the craftsmen were rude and lawless, and any petty event was sufficient to bring out a band and cause a "tuilzie," or street fight. King James VI. abhorred these outbreaks and wrote in words which are well known : "the craftsmen think we should be content with their work, how bad and dear soever it be, and if they in any thing be controlled, up goeth the blew blanket."

Opposition also came from the Town Council, no doubt for the reason that that body was under the control of the merchants. There was perhaps good reason for the suspicion that the trades imposed on the neighbours by turning out inferior handiwork and charging exorbitant prices. It was in vain that all craftsmen were required by Act of Parliament "to mak gude and sufficient stuff and sell the same at ane competent price." The Town Council, acting in the public interest, had to control the new bodies and insist on some system of internal discipline. By degrees the craftsmen became more numerous and more respectable, their Incorporations received official recognition, and they were allotted a number of seats in the Town Council. These Incorporations were formed on the model of the Merchant Guild ; their objects were to provide for the performance of religious rites, for self-government within their respective spheres, and for charity towards their poor members. Between the middle of the fifteenth and the end of the sixteenth century the Town Council granted Charters, called Seals of

The Incorporations

Cause, to fourteen Incorporations in Edinburgh. In so acting the Town Council had no authority from Parliament or the Crown; but they assumed the power to regulate the crafts in this way as being an administrative act and for the purpose of promoting civic harmony and the business interests of the burgh. In these Seals of Cause each craft was taken bound to support an altar in St Giles' Church to its patron saint; each obtained a monopoly within its own domain and protection from competition; and rules were provided for the discipline of the members, and the admission of apprentices.

The fourteen Incorporations thus set up were the following:—bonnetmakers, skinners, furriers, cordiners, tailors, fleshers, wrights, masons, baxters, hammermen, goldsmiths, weavers, waulkers, and surgeons. It is a singular indication of the persistence of institutions in Edinburgh that these Incorporations still continue to exist. The waulkers were at an early date united with the bonnetmakers; the surgeons were formerly united with the barbers, but in 1778 they were incorporated again under the title of the Royal College of Surgeons. The other twelve Incorporations are no longer concerned with old monopolies or the standard of the workmanship turned out by their members, but are merely benefit societies with a limited membership more exclusive by far than anything ever conceived by the ancient Merchant Guild. They combine to elect the Convener of Trades, who represents them in the Town

The Freedom of the City

Council and is the last of the "chains," and is traditionally assigned a seat opposite to the Lord Provost as being Vice-Preses in the Council meetings. This arrangement is mentioned in a Town Council Minute of date 6th December 1780.

While the Guild and the Incorporations had their several spheres within which they were free to operate, **The Admission of Burgesses.** they were still in a general sense subject to the control of the Town Council. Thus the Town Council fixed the prices of bread, fish, flesh, ale and other commodities, and appointed markets and days and hours of sale; and they might approve or disapprove of any regulations proposed by any of the bodies. It was the Town Council who admitted the burgesses and fixed the terms and conditions of this ceremony; and no one could become a member of any incorporation or practise any craft until he had been made a burgess.

The Town Clerk kept a Register of Burgesses and Guild Brethren of the City, and this Register is fortunately complete since 17th May 1487 and is contained in a series of twenty-two volumes. Recently the Scottish Record Society has published a Roll of Edinburgh Burgesses for the period 1406 to 1700, edited by Mr Boog Watson.

The fees paid by new burgesses at their admission have all along formed part of the burgh revenues. An old Act provided that the "proffit that is tane for the making of ilk burges or gilde brother be put to the common gude and warit on the common warkis." It is not surprising that this subject is frequently mentioned in the Council Minutes. In March 1507-8 the rates were fixed as follows:—the heir of a burgess paid 6s. 8d. for burgess-ship and 13s. 4d. for guildry; other sons and daughters paid 13s. 4d. for burgess-ship and 20s. for guildry; unfreemen paid £3 for burgess-ship and £5 for guildry. In 1508 one person was admitted burgess, thirty-one were admitted guild brethren, and seventeen were admitted burgesses and guild brethren. In 1564 the duties payable by the unfreemen were raised to £20 for burgess-ship and £40 for guildry without prejudice to the rights of burgess' bairns, and in that year fifty-six persons were enrolled as burgesses, three as guild brethren, and twelve as burgesses and guild brethren. In 1602 the rates for strangers went much higher, being 100 merks for burgess-ship and £100 for guildry; in 1647 these figures were increased to £160 and £240 respectively, scots money. In the latter part of the following century a stranger paid £12, 10s. sterling for burgess-ship, and £25 when admitted burgess and guild brother; and those who entered in right of a father, or wife, or master, paid half of these amounts. In some years the revenue from this source exceeded £1000. In the middle of last century the fees for burgesses were the following:—for strangers, £16, 9s.; for apprentices, £8; for burgess' bairns, £6, 5s. 6d.

The burgesses were required by various Acts

of Parliament to be armed and harnessed according to their means and to attend weapon-showings four times a year and go through military exercises at the sight of the Provost and Bailies. The Town Council also required merchants and craftsmen to have in their booths "ane axe or twa or thre aftir as thay haif servandis"; and to come incontinent to the aid of the Magistrates when required. On 4th March 1552-3 the Council, having regard to the great slaughters and tulzies in the burgh, required the merchants and craftsmen to have long weapons in their booths or chambers and to come forth on the ringing of the common bell for "stanching thairof." In 1567 the Town Council ordained that every man at the making of him burgess should oblige himself to have "speir, sword, buklar and steill bonet for serving of the baillies and gude toun quhen thai haif ado." In 1588 the Council ordained that no burgess be received or admitted in time coming but such as should compear at the time of his admission before the Council with "sufficient airmour" and make faith that the same was his own proper gear. In 1591 the Town Council ordained that any one being made a burgess must be sufficiently armed "with ane furnisht muskitt." This simple requirement held good from 1591 to 1644, and the printed Roll of Burgesses indicates that those admitted in this period generally produced a "muskitt." Thereafter a sum was added to the entry money as "arms silver," the amount in 1654 being £16; and the money raised in this way was laid out by the Dean of Guild in buying arms for the town's magazine. This practice was continued until the end of the seventeenth century.

Every burgess at his admission had to take an oath, which was added to from time to time so that it became almost a creed in itself. He swore to be leal and true to the King and to the Provost and Bailies; to underlie and keep the laws of the burgh; and to obey the officers of the burgh. "In all taxations, watching, warding and all uther charges to be layet upon the burgh I sall willinglie beir my pairt with the rest of the nichtbours as I am commandit thairto be the magistratis and officeris of the burgh." After the Reformation he had to profess the "trew religion" and to abjure the Roman faith "callit papistry."

The guild brother had also to take an oath requiring him to give his best counsel to the burgh; not to dispone the common good but for the common profit; to make concord to the best of his power; and to give leal and true judgment on all occasions.

It will be remembered that one of the Secession churches in the eighteenth century divided into two parts on the subject of the burgess oath, one section becoming known as the burghers and the other section as the anti-burghers.

In the year 1819 the subject was raised in the Town Council, upon a recommendation of the Convention of Burghs, that the burgess oath should be dispensed with; and it was stated that it had already gone into complete desuetude in Edinburgh.

In former times trade and industry in Scotland were conducted on a personal or domestic basis, and factories did not exist. The word "merchant" did not mean a wholesale trader, but rather a shopkeeper; and this use survives in the common expression of "grocer and provision merchant." A craftsman was a mechanic or artisan who made goods to order and not for stock. When it happened that he had a surplus for sale this was put on the market, not by the craftsman, but by a merchant, the two functions being separate and distinct. The unit of the family was important, the typical burgess being a person with a residence in the burgh and the head of a household. Hence at different times the Town Council ordained that burgesses should be married men and should reside in the burgh or forfeit their freedom. In 1555 they passed an Act which provided that no person should be received or admitted burgess "except honest qualifyit men, and that thai be maryit, dwelland within the burgh, haiffand sufficient substance, with stob and staik." A few years later they refused to admit a person of some consequence because he was a bachelor. He was required to apply again when he had "ane lawful wyfe and mariit according to the ordour of the Kirk," upon which his petition would be considered and satisfied.

The apprentice of a craftsman required to have

a formal indenture and to have his name "bookit" in proper form. When his term of five or seven years was completed and he was seeking to become a burgess he had to produce his indenture and a "testification of his good and true service during all the years of his bondage"; whereupon he was admitted on payment of certain dues. But the apprentice in former days was expected to marry his master's daughter, and only by doing so could he hope for admission on the most favourable terms. This subject was elaborated at length in a Minute of the year 1585, which shows the Town Council as interfering unduly in matrimonial matters; "to move thame to tak in marriage thair maister's dochteris before any utheris quhilk sall be ane greitt comfort and support to friemen, that thairfore no prenteis be resavit burges without he haif servit after the ish of his prenteischip ane frieman for the space of thrie yeir for meitt and fie." He was then to be received burgess, and five years later he might become guild brother; but if he married according to orders he might become burgess and guild brother "at any time be rycht of his wyfe."

The Town Council put down with a heavy hand all those who sought to enjoy the privileges of freedom without being admitted thereto in due and proper form. They could fine or imprison such unruly persons or confiscate their goods. In 1551 the Dean of Guild was ordered to shut up the doors of the booths of all persons who were not freemen, and not to allow them to occupy any kind of freedom until they had paid the duty therefor. In 1580, two bookbinders lodged a complaint against a stranger and unfreeman who usurped the freedom of the burgh in binding and selling books "to the greitt hurt and prejudice of the compleners quha ar burgesses and friemen, quha stents, watches, and wardes and beirs all uther portabill charges with the nychtbouris of the burgh, quhilk thai ar nocht abill to do gif the said unfreeman be sufferit to continue in the said tred." The party accused appeared before the Town Council and was discharged from binding books within the burgh under pain of confiscation thereof. This case is typical of many appearing in the Council Records.

The system of monopolies no doubt arose out of the early conditions of burghal life, and presumably it was tolerated so long as it suited the ideas and needs of the people. It began to break down in the eighteenth century; and, although the theory was maintained by decisions of the Law Courts, it was recognised that the virtue had gone out of it, and the system was confined within narrowing limits and under conditions which were increasingly artificial. One of the last remnants of trading benefits was the reduced rates charged on goods imported by burgesses into Leith. Another benefit, unconnected with trade, which continued down to modern times was the preference given to burgesses

Reforms

in connection with Trinity Hospital and the admission of their children to Heriot's Hospital.

In 1833 the Burgh Reform Act was passed. This Act granted to the guildry the free election

Changes in Last Century. of the Dean of Guild, thus reversing in Edinburgh a practice which had prevailed since the fifteenth century. The guildry began again to hold meetings and asserted a right to elect the members and officials of the Dean of Guild Court. This attitude opened up a variety of possibilities which naturally caused some perturbation in the Town Council and led them to seek an interdict in Court, whereupon the claim was abandoned. The claim of the guildry was not without precedent, as in Glasgow the Dean of Guild Court is controlled by the Trades House and not by the Town Council.

In 1846 an Act was passed which abolished all exclusive privileges in dealing with merchandise or exercising trades and handicrafts. "It shall be lawful for any person to carry on or deal in merchandise and to carry on or exercise any trade or handicraft in any burgh and elsewhere in Scotland without being a burgess of such burgh or a guild brother or a member of any guild, craft, or incorporation."

The question of burgess dues was under the consideration of the Town Council on various occasions. In the early part of last century the Merchant Company were desirous to extend their

73

membership beyond the limits of the city. They proposed to apply to Parliament for power to dispense with the condition which required their members to be burgesses and guild brethren; which seems to indicate a disregard of past history, and would have been an unfortunate breach of their traditions. The dues of burgess-ship were then considerable, and tickets were only given to traders or householders in the city. The Town Council, however, arranged to depart from the latter condition, and it is no longer necessary for applicants to have any local or property qualification when they enter either the Merchant Company or a trade incorporation. Other applicants must produce receipts vouching the payment of burgh rates for three years; so that any occupant of premises within the city for this short period is nowadays a potential burgess and guild brother. Since the year 1881 the fee has been fixed at 21s. with, in addition, a sum of 2s. 6d. payable to the guildry. There have been various Acts of Parliament dealing with the qualification for burgesses, the latest being the Town Council Act of 1900.

The Town Council no longer exercise any jurisdiction over the incorporations, but the affairs of these bodies occasionally come under the notice of the Law Courts. In 1912 the Incorporation of Tailors were in the Court of Session because of a difficulty arising from the fact that the membership was then reduced to one person who sought to

entail the funds of the body upon his own family.
To this, however, the Court would not consent.
In 1911 the Incorporation of Cordiners presented
to the Court a scheme to regulate the admission of
new members. The old distinction was preserved
between burgess' bairns and strangers, the former
being designated entrants "at the near hand" and
the latter entrants "at the far hand." For the
former class a scale was fixed which varied from
£178, 10s. to £189; for the latter class a scale was
fixed varying from £720 to £1620. The Court was
apparently satisfied that these formidable fees were
warranted and the scheme was approved.

In the ordinary case the Town Council bestowed
the freedom of the burgh upon applicants who
Gratis complied with their conditions, one of
Burgesses. these being the payment of a certain
amount to the common good. It seems that the
common good was administered partly by the
Treasurer and partly by the Dean of Guild; and
the burgess money belonged to the Dean of
Guild to be wared by him on the repair of the
churches. But the grant of the freedom was
always within the discretion of the Town Council,
and all along there have been occasions when they
put aside their regulations and made the grant freely
and by way of gift. Sometimes this was done as
a reward or favour, sometimes at the request of
the King or a nobleman whom the Town Council
found it convenient to conciliate. These grants

were known as gratis burgess-ships, and in the early
Records they seldom assume an honorary character
but were generally made to persons who would use
the privileges attached to them and trade as a
merchant or exercise a craft; but where it is
practically certain that the grantee had no such
intention, it may be supposed that the freedom was
conferred as an honour. At a later date a distinction was recognised between gratis and honorary
burgesses.

Early in the history of the burgh the Town
Council granted to the Provost a freedom of guildry
to be given by him to whomsoever he pleased. A
Minute of 5th January 1570-1 narrates that in times
past, the Provost, Bailies, and other officers of the
burgh, by right of their offices, had certain burgess-
ships "quhilks thai disponit at thair plesour."
Another Minute, of date 23rd September 1687,
narrates that the Lord Provost had during each
year of his office the admission of two burgesses
and guild brethren; and each Bailie, Dean of Guild,
and Treasurer had the admission of one; and that
they were in the habit of selling these admissions
and appropriating the proceeds. This led to abuses,
and in the years 1715 and 1716 the Town Council
passed resolutions to end the practice, and instructed
the Dean of Guild to pay £200 yearly to the
Lord Provost, and £100 to each of the Magistrates
"in lieu of their tickets." An unusual Minute of
25th March 1724 mentions that the Clerk had signed

four burgess and guild-brethren tickets and sent them to the Lord Provost in London to be filled up by him as he should think fit.

There are many instances of burgesses made at the request of the sovereign or noblemen " because sic requests cannot commounlie be refusit for eschewing of the displesour of the said greit men and courteours." In 1556 one case is mentioned where the request came from the Queen. In 1563 a taverner was made burgess and guild brother gratis at the request of the Abbot of St Colme's Inch. In 1568 two cases are mentioned, one at the request of the Earl of Mar, the other at the request of the Lord Regent. In 1579 an embroiderer was admitted at the King's request; in 1581 the master cook of the King was admitted; in 1582 a surgeon was admitted at the request of Lord Bothwell; in 1584 the servant of the Archbishop of St Andrews was admitted; in 1590 a chapman at the request of David M'Gill, King's Advocate. The list could be extended indefinitely, and it is presumed that these individuals meant to put their freedom to practical purposes.

The persons admitted gratis by way of favour or reward were not so numerous. In 1556 a certain wright who had been seriously injured in the work of the town received compensation in this form. In 1562 two masons were admitted for their work on the Tolbooth, and in 1586 a party was so rewarded for good service in time of

pestilence. The citizen who played the part of
Robin Hood in the May games seems to have
had the right to be admitted a burgess gratis.

During the occupation by Cromwell, the Town
Council freely admitted not only the English
soldiers, but also the English civilians who settled
in this locality. In 1655 the Bailies met with
some of the officers of the garrison, and half a
dozen tickets were "disponed upon at the discretion
of the said officers and themselves." In 1656 not
only the English officers but their "followers"
were admitted gratis, the Town Council no doubt
having good reason to make free with their favours
in this way. In 1663, after the Restoration, the
Town Council resolved to give a "kindly welcome"
to the Members of Parliament and other persons
of quality returning to the town, and to admit
them and "sume of thair servants and followers"
to the freedom of the burgh. In fact, about this
time the system appears to have got out of hand,
and it became necessary to make some regulation
as it was complained that the gratis burgesses were
taking up callings and bidding fair to "eat the
meat out of the freemen's mouths." It was therefore provided by various Minutes that gratis
burgesses should have the privilege for themselves
only and not for their children; that they should
have no benefit of taking apprentices or right
of admission to hospitals; should have "no
place of the good town" nor be qualified to bear

any public office. The whole practice in relation
to gratis burgesses of this description seems to
have died out about the middle of the eighteenth
century; and the expression ceased to be used.
Thereafter the freedom of the city was gifted by
the Town Council, not for the material benefits
attaching thereto, but on rare occasions to persons
of distinction who were designated honorary
burgesses.

From an early period cases are mentioned in
the Minutes of persons admitted as burgesses who
Honorary Burgesses. would not be likely to engage in
trade, or were not resident in Edin-
burgh. These were notable personages, generally
noblemen or officials of high rank, and so it may
be concluded that the gift was intended to be a
compliment from the Town Council. There seems,
therefore, to be good reason for assuming that the
institution of honorary burgesses dates back as far as
the extant Records of the city.

On 3rd October 1459, Sir Edward Boncle was
made a brother of the guild gratis "for his aid
and counsel." He was the first Provost of
Trinity College. On 30th September 1513, Master
Gavin Douglas, Provost of the collegiate church
of St Giles, was made a burgess gratis "for the
common benefit of the town." In 1557, the
Seigneur d'Oysel was made a burgess and guild
brother by the gift of the Town Council. He was
French Ambassador at the Court of the Queen

Regent, and Lieutenant-General of the French forces in Scotland. Other instances are the following:—In 1567, Sir James Balfour of Pittindreich, Clerk Register; in 1597, John Brand, minister of the Canongate; in 1598, Alexander, Lord Urquhart and Fyvie; in 1604, John, Lord Thirlestane, from whom the reversion of Leith was bought; in 1613, the Bishops of St Andrews and Glasgow, and the Lord President; in 1616, the Duke of Lennox; in 1617, the noblemen and gentlemen who accompanied King James on his journey to Scotland; in 1618, Ben Jonson; in 1626, the Marquess of Hamilton and the Earl of Cassilis; in 1632, the Earl Marischal and Lord Kinpont.

The gifts were in some cases recognitions of services done to the burgh or to the nation; in other cases they commemorated events of local or general importance. But in the seventeenth century they seem also to represent the trend of national history, the Town Council following and responding to the prevailing opinions, whatever these might be, so that the lists of honorary burgesses reflect and vary with the domination of parties in Scotland.

In the latter part of the reign of King James VI. the Town Council, apparently anxious to stand well with the King, honoured his new bishops in this way. In 1640, they admitted General Alexander Leslie; in 1641, the noblemen and gentlemen in attendance on King Charles at the banquet given to him; in 1644, Sir Harry Vane; in 1647, Thomas

The Influence of Politics

Cunningham, Conservator at Campvere who had supplied arms to the Scottish Army ; in 1648, Sir Archibald Johnston of Warriston and other Scottish leaders.

From 1650 to 1657 the admissions reflect the English occupation. Nicoll records in his Diary that on 14th August 1656 the town of Edinburgh feasted Lord Broghill, Great President of the Council of Scotland, with the General of the army of Monk, as also the whole persons of the Council of State and likewise the officers and commanders of the army, the judges of the land and their followers. The feast was given, he says, with great solemnity in the Parliament House, richly hung for that end. The "hail pryme" men and such of their followers as were in respect were all "resavit burgessis and thair burges tickettis delyverit to thaim."

After the death of the Lord Protector, there were indications of the turning tide and the Restoration saw a revival of the practice of admitting members of the nobility and gentry, not only in individual cases, but almost in battalions. It is also mentioned on some of the occasions that the parties to be honoured in this way were invited to banquets. Further, an Act of the Town Council ordered all burgess tickets to be written in the King's name, and such as had been admitted during the "usurpation" were ordered to appear and show their tickets, an order which the irreconcilables would be certain to disregard. In 1660 the Earl of Glencairn and ten other noblemen were admitted on a certain day; and in the following year another company of noblemen were admitted, including the Earl of Atholl. In 1663, at the meeting of Parliament, the Town Council considered that there would be a "necessity to gratifie those in publick authoritie and uther personis of qualitie by giving to them a kyndlie welcome to the towne and be admitting them and sume of their servants and followers to the freedome of this burgh." They accordingly gave power to the Lord Provost to perform these things "in the most decent and frugall way." In 1665 the Town Council passed an Act under which they resolved to admit all the ministers of the burgh to be burgesses and guild brethren "in best forme." In 1679 the Duke of Buccleuch and Monmouth was admitted and the burgess ticket was on that occasion delivered in a "gold box." This seems to have been the first occasion when a box, or casket as it is now termed, was made use of in connection with the ceremony.

In 1679 the Duke of York (afterwards King James VII.) came to reside in the Palace of Holyrood, and upon his entry into Edinburgh he was received with great pomp and was magnificently entertained by the citizens. One entertainment given to him and the Duchess and their Court in the Parliament House is said to have cost the town £1400 sterling, and on that occasion he and one hundred and twenty-three of his attendants were presented with the freedom of the city.

Position at the Revolution

In 1684 the Lord Chancellor and thirty-nine Drummonds were made burgesses and guild brethren by Act of the Town Council. In 1685 the Town Council ordained that all the bishops not already burgesses should be admitted gratis. In 1687 the Town Council appointed the principal and whole professors and regents of the College to be received gratis. In 1687, when the policy of King James was turning towards Roman Catholicism, the Town Council presented the freedom to the Rector of the Scots College in Paris, and to the Colonel of the English Gendarmes belonging to the King of France's Life Guards.

The Revolution of 1689 had not any marked influence in the matter of honorary burgesses, except that for a number of years thereafter very few cases are recorded. A Minute of the Town Council, of date 27th March 1700, mentions that considerable sums had been paid to the clerks for burgess tickets given gratis. Therefore they appointed the parties to be favoured in this way to pay the Clerk's dues "as others do pay, excepting allways such noblemen and gentilmen as the councill shall think fitt to complement with the freedome of this city." In 1701 the Town Council ordered that a list should be kept of gratis burgesses, but this, if ever made, has disappeared.

Thereafter the Minutes record the admission of numerous great personages including the following :—
In 1704, the Duke of Argyll ; in 1707, Sir John Cope ;

in 1708, Admiral Byng and the Earl of Lauderdale ; in 1714, the Duke of Queensberry and the Duke of Douglas. In 1716, after the troubles of the Jacobite Rebellion, the Commissary-General and a number of officers of the army were admitted, presumably in recognition of their services to the Government. In 1719 the honour was given to John Law of Lauriston, and again in this case the ticket was enclosed in a gold box.

In 1729 a Minute of the Town Council mentioned that considerable sums had been expended annually upon entertainments "at the making of noblemen, gentlemen and others burgesses which by no means the toun was able to bear." Therefore it was ordained that for the future no entertainment should be given at the town's charge on such occasions, "excepting allenarly all such as are His Majestie's ministers of State and his Majestie's judges of the Court of Session and Exchequer, the Commander in Chief of His Majestie's forces in North Britain, in which event the Town Council shall not only authorise the freedome of the burgh to be given to the persons above excepted, but shall order and authorize the entertainment on that occasion." In 1731 another Minute distinguished between gratis tickets given to servants of Commissioners of the General Assembly and such like, and "honorary tickets that are given in complement to noblemen and gentlemen."

In 1745 the following were admitted :—The Earl

of Loudon, Lord Banff, Colonel Campbell and
other officers. In 1747 the Earl of Albemarle was
admitted. He succeeded the Duke of Cumberland
as commander of the forces in Scotland, and
received thanks for his good services. Among
other notabilities the following names occur:—In
1759, Benjamin Franklin of Philadelphia and his son ;
in 1760, Dr Tobias Smollett and the Rev. George
Whitefield ; in 1766, the Archbishop of York.

In 1764 the Town Council ordered again that a
Register of Honorary Burgesses should be kept.
This seems to have been done for some years but this
Register has also been lost. A Minute of the Town
Council of date 13th May 1767 seems to be of
importance for the reason that it states the principles
which should regulate the granting of the freedom :
"Considering that the practice has for some time
prevailed of giving the freedom of the city to many
persons indiscriminately, which has been attended
with great inconvenience, the Council do therefore
enact and declare that no burges ticket shall be
granted in time coming to any person whomever but
such as are invested with public character or shall
have signalized himself in the service of his country
or this city." It may be said that this Minute is
still operative in the sense that the principles stated
therein are in accordance with the modern practice
of the Town Council, and there seems to be no
pronouncement or regulation of later date. After
this date the following admissions occurred:—In

1767, Dr Alexander Carlyle of Inveresk; in 1770, Adam Smith; in 1772, Thomas Pennant; in 1775, Hugo Arnot; in 1780, Admiral Sir George Bridges Rodney (with the ticket in a gold box); in 1781, Admiral Parker and his captains; in 1791, Robert Adam, architect; in 1804, Dr Jenner; in 1809, Sir David Baird. It is mentioned that the cost of an elegant gold box about this date was £105.

The only Register known to exist, dates from 1813. It contains columns for names, statements of reasons, dates and signatures. It is the custom now for honorary burgesses to sign the Register at the freedom ceremony, but this practice only dates from 1853 when Mr Gladstone received the freedom and signed what is known as the Burgess Roll. Between 1813 and 1900 this Roll contains 129 names, including the following:—Walter Scott, 1813; Gilbert Innes of Stow, 1814; Marquess of Bute, 1815; Dr James Gregory, 1815; Archdukes John and Lewis of Austria, 1815; the Grand Duke Nicolas of Russia, 1816; Grand Duke Michael of Russia, 1818; Prince Leopold, 1819; Prince Victor of Matternich, 1821; Earl of Lauderdale, 1824; Henry Brougham, 1825; David Wilkie, R.A., 1829; Earl Grey, 1834; Sir Thomas M. Brisbane, 1834; Thomas Campbell, 1836; Thomas Babington Macaulay, 1839; Charles Dickens, 1841; William Gibson Craig, 1841; The Prince Consort, 1842; Duke of Buccleuch, 1842; Sir Robert Peel, 1842; Earl of Aberdeen, 1842; Richard Cobden, 1843; Lord John Russell, 1845;

Great Men

Sir Charles Napier, 1845; W. E. Gladstone, 1853; Marquess of Dalhousie, 1856; Rev. David Livingstone, 1857; David Roberts, R.A., 1858; Viscount Palmerston, 1863; General Garibaldi, 1864; Prince Alfred, 1866; William Lloyd Garrison, 1867; Benjamin Disraeli, 1867; Lord Napier of Magdala, 1868; Sir James Y. Simpson, 1869; John Bright, 1869; Baroness Burdett Coutts, 1874; Ex-President Grant, U.S.A., 1877; Earl of Shaftesbury, 1878; Marquess of Salisbury, 1882; Earl of Rosebery, 1883; Earl of Aberdeen, 1885; Prince Albert Victor, 1886; Marquess of Lothian, 1887; Andrew Carnegie, 1887; Henry M. Stanley, 1890; Sir Daniel Wilson, 1891; Duke of York, 1893; Lord Roberts, 1893; Earl of Elgin, 1893; Earl of Hopetoun, 1895; John Ritchie Findlay, 1896; William M'Ewan, 1897; Lord Wolseley, 1898; Lord Lister, 1898; Marquess of Dufferin, 1898; General Kitchener, 1898; Albert Edward, Prince of Wales, 1899.

CHAPTER IV

CROMWELL AND LEITH

THE chapter of Edinburgh history which is associated with the name of Cromwell has been dealt with by many writers, and, as it happens, a large number of papers of the period have been preserved in the City Chambers. These papers do not add anything to the general facts already well known, but they contain an amount of information on local subjects, chiefly connected with Leith, which has not so far been made available to the public. Local historians have referred to the fact that at this time the age-long controversy was still being waged between Edinburgh and Leith, but they have given no details, although these have a certain value as showing the ideas then prevailing in respect of trading rights and local government. Again it seems, oddly enough, to be the case that less is known about the Citadel built by Cromwell in Leith than about the great forts constructed by him in other parts of Scotland ; and no plan of the former is known to exist. Upon both of these topics the City Records contain information, though perhaps on matters of detail only. It is proposed here to give quotations from some of the papers, and to refer to certain others which appear to be of some interest.

A few days after the Battle of Dunbar in 1650, Cromwell arrived in Edinburgh and took up his **Cromwell's** quarters in Moray House in the **Visit.** Canongate, where he remained for about a year. The Lord Provost and Magistrates had fled to Stirling, but, after some negotiations and delay, they were permitted to return and resume their functions. Leith had been occupied by some regiments under Major-General Lambert, and an endeavour was made to improve the fortified works in existence at the port. "We found in it mounted on platforms 37 guns, some shott and ammunition and great store of wealth." When Cromwell returned to England, he left behind him General Monk as commander of the forces in Scotland, and for a time Monk was located in Leith, where he maintained a large permanent garrison, making this place his headquarters in Scotland. After the example of the Edinburgh Magistrates there had been an exodus from the port; the South Leith Records mention that "after the defeat at Dunbar the ministers and most part of all ye honest people fled out of the town for fear of ye enemie." The church and churchyard of South Leith and some buildings in the neighbourhood were occupied by the English forces as a "magasin."

Cromwell endeavoured to win over the Scots for the Commonwealth, but the English were aware that the Leithers were ready to rise against them, and in particular the ministers were regarded as "trumpets of sedition." Cromwell's difficulties in Scotland arose almost entirely from the clergy, who were firmly attached to the cause of the monarchy. When they preached, great numbers attended their services, particularly in Leith. Writing about South Leith in 1655, Monk stated that the preachings there were dangerous because there was "so great a resort of Scottish men that there would be above 1000 of them there on the Lord's day, which I thought not safe to suffer any longer, the magazine wherein our arms and ammunition is being so neare." In 1656 the parishioners of South Leith were ordered to worship in the North Kirk "until the magasin be removit from ye south paroch into ye citadel." The embargo was not removed until June 1657, when the Citadel in North Leith had been erected and occupied.

While Monk was resident in Leith he induced some English families of considerable wealth to settle in Leith, by whom, it is said, the glass industry was introduced into this area, and who otherwise gave an impulse to the mercantile spirit of the port. These traders speedily became aware of the fact that Leith was an unfree place, and that in matters of trade they were subject to minute regulation from the Royal Burgh of Edinburgh, the dominant owners of the harbour and the feudal superiors of the town. No doubt they discussed these and other grievances

with General Monk, who, at first taking their part,
declared that Leith was under the "greatest slavery
that ever I knew." In a letter to the Protector, of
date 18th January 1654, Monk wrote regarding the
English who had settled in Leith, " by Your Highness'
encouragement . . . I humbly desire that if it should
not be thought fit that Leith shall have the like
privileges that other corporations in the three
nations have, that yet there may be some bounds set
to the authority of the city of Edinburgh over them
so that the Englishmen may not be enforced wholly
to remove themselves from the town where their
residence hath been found by experience not only to
conduce much to the public interest in general but
to the strengthening of the garrison." In a further
letter to the Protector, dated 14th February 1654,
Monk referred again to the condition of the
merchants and other inhabitants of Leith, both
English and Scottish, on account of the superiority
which the City of Edinburgh claimed to have over
them, and to the burdens which Edinburgh imposed
"by their unbounded authority," which obstructed
trade and occasioned the English to quit the town ;
" for the redress of which and many other grievances
and inconveniences they have desired Captain
Newman to attend Your Highness and Council,
by whom I have presumed to recommend to your
Highness to grant such a favorable answer to their
proposals as may encurrage the English to continue
in that town and garrison, by having liberty to chuse

their own Magistrates and enjoy the privileges of a Corporation during the time it is a garrison."

Being encouraged by General Monk and relying upon his powerful aid, the merchants and inhabitants of Leith resolved in the year 1655 to submit their claims to the Protector as head of the republican government, and with this end in view they prepared a formal Petition containing their case. The Petition was followed by Answers from the Town Council of Edinburgh; and by other voluminous papers grouped together in the City Records as "The Writs relating to the great struggle and contest betwixt the Town of Edinburgh and Leith anent the superiority of Leith before Oliver Cromwell and his Council."

This controversy is centuries old, and it may be hoped that the parties to these old, unhappy, far-off things may recall the details with the dispassionate feelings and the interest which we experience in reading about the old wars of Scotland and England. The desire of the people of Leith was to enjoy and possess equal rights and privileges with their more favoured neighbours, but Edinburgh was most unwilling to grant this concession. The ambitions of Leith were perhaps premature in view of the medieval conceptions then prevailing, but, if they had been realised in 1655, an identity of interests would have been established for the two places, a consummation which was only attained in the year 1920.

Petition to the Protector

The Petition was addressed to His Highness Oliver, Lord Protector, from the merchants, traders **The Petition** and inhabitants of Leith, setting forth **of Leith.** that the sad condition and most grievous oppressions they lay under by the Magistrates of Edinburgh forced them to apply to His Highness for redress. The Petition then proceeded to state as follows:—

That they having formerly chosen their own magistrates once a year and by them ordered their own affairs, were then denied that liberty by the magistrates of Edinburgh (whose malice was so great to the interest of the English nation); that they not only imposed rulers over them, but also laid what arbitrary and unlimited taxes they pleased upon their lands and houses, altering their charters and evidents at their pleasure; exacted a merk Scots upon every tun of their goods imported, which in many commodities was more than the State's Customs; forcing as many as had valuable estates to leave their houses at Leith and to live in Edinburgh where they had neither houses, friends nor customers; and if they brought in any commodities to the port they were not permitted to sell any of them until they proffered them to the Town Council of Edinburgh, who usually held them in suspense for an answer sixteen or twenty days together, on purpose that other ships might arrive, and the Petitioners might lose the benefit of their adventures.

The said Magistrates had set up a public weigh house, forcing all men to bring in their goods and pay one penny sterling per cent. for weighing them, although they had lawful weights of their own; which weigh house they farmed out to Edinburgh merchants so that the Petitioners could sell no goods but they must know their customers.

They compelled all who sold wine and beer, maltmakers and brewers, to pay them a yearly duty and limited them to what number they pleased. For every tun of wine that went from Leith to Edinburgh they exacted one pound thirteen shillings and fourpence sterling, and fourpence per pound weight upon tobacco and for strong waters and other commodities; which said tax they were laying on and exacting from the Petitioners.

They laid high imposition upon ballast for ships, anchorage, shore dues, &c., which with many other oppressions had driven away most of all the English merchants who did in time of freedom of trade resort thither; and they had forty ships arrived there for one since these impositions, as the Commissioners of the Customs and their books would testify; for rather than come with their ships and goods to Leith they would go to other ports and there get their goods ashore, so that not only the trade was lost but the Commonwealth defrauded.

They had got also an excise upon beer and ale which they laid upon malt, forcing the Petitioners to pay near the third part of their malt, refusing them the liberty of a market, which (the town of Leith being a garrison) was very prejudicial.

They were forcing the Petitioners of the Scots nation to pay such cesses as were laid on six or seven years past; and were indebted to the

Petition to the Protector

Petitioners near three thousand pounds sterling for billeting soldiers which they, to ease themselves, sent to the Petitioners and afterwards sent their drums about the town, desiring all men to bring in their "bilgates" and they should be paid, which, when they had received, they got the monies from the Committee of Estates and never paid the Petitioners.

To omit very many other oppressions they exercised over the Petitioners, whatever place whereof any money could be possibly raised, that they collected and carried to their treasury at Edinburgh, with which they maintained their agents in England to keep up their oppressions over the Petitioners at home, so that the Petitioners had not the public revenue to carry on the affairs of the town, such as to maintain their poor, repair their churches, pave the streets, &c. And for want of faithful magistrates to rule and act amongst them, no effectual care was taken that brewers, butchers, bakers and vintners did conform themselves to the laws, nor lewd persons corrected but by the care of the Governor.

That in respect several of the Petitioners were many years since encouraged by his Highness' Order to the present Governor and the Commissioners in Scotland to leave their habitations, trades and nearest relations in England and to live in Leith, and had, since their abode, there engaged against the arbitrary power and unlimited oppressions of the late Tyrant his person and friends. And for that end the Petitioners had also assisted with their ships for transporting soldiers and provisions to the islands and garrisons adjacent and drawn out one hundred horse at a time to assist the Governor, when the army was in the hills and the enemy round the Petitioners, and done other remarkable services for the Commonwealth. And in respect the said magistrates of Edinburgh had no law, custom or privilege for their unreasonable oppressions, which being over their fellow subjects were against the law of God, nature and nations, and were not paralleled by any city or incorporation in Europe.

THEREFORE the petitioners humbly prayed that his Highness would be pleased to break the heavy yokes of their oppressors; to set the Petitioners free and give them protection under his Government by empowering them to incorporate themselves and choose their own magistrates yearly; to take off all the grievances before mentioned exercised over them by the magistrates of Edinburgh; that the petty receipts of the town, as ballast, shore-dues and anchorage might go towards carrying on the public affairs of the town and building an almshouse for maintenance of English soldiers maimed in the Scots service, and other English that might be reduced to great necessity; and that Leith might be made equally free with other ports in his Highness's Dominions.

On the back of this Petition there is the following Deliverance :—

"WHITEHALL the 26th June 1655: We do refer the consideration of this Petition of the inhabitants of the town of Leith, with their paper of grievances hereunto annexed, unto General Monk, whom we do desire and authorize (calling to his assistance any two of the Judges in Scotland) to hear and examine all the matters complained of in the said Petition, and the differences between the inhabitants of the City of Edinburgh and the said inhabitants of Leith, and to endeavour to compose the same (if they can) or otherways to certify unto us the true state thereof, together with their opinion concerning the same.

(Signed)   OLIVER P."

The Magistrates and Council of Edinburgh prepared and gave in Answers " to the pretended The Answers of grievances and petition of those who Edinburgh. called themselves merchants traders and inhabitants of Leith, presented to His Highness the Lord Protector and by him referred to General Monk, calling to his assistance any two of the judges in Scotland." This document unfortunately is so lengthy that only a résumé of its contents can be attempted.

Before entering upon particular Answers the Town Council made some observations concerning the state and liberty of the free burghs of Scotland in general and of their own burgh in its relation to the village of Leith, these being to the effect following :—(1) That the Royal burghs were one of the estates of Parliament endowed by Parliament and by the Scottish Kings with grants " whereby it was most evident that the privileges and freedoms of burghs were ever carefully guarded and that none dwelling without free burgh or not being free burgesses

should use any sort of merchandise nor tapp and
sell wine, wax, silk, spiceries nor any such like
commodities under the pain of confiscation of their
whole moveables." (2) That freemen only, indwellers
within royal burghs, should enjoy the said liberties.
(3) That the burghs had also power to charge unfreemen; usurpers of the liberties of burghs, to find caution
for their obedience to the Acts against unfreemen.
(4) That no person of whatever degree was permitted
to molest or trouble the magistrates of burghs and
merchants thereof in using their liberties and privileges. (5) That all kinds of merchandise should be
presented and offered to be sold within the burgh
and not without the same.

Passing from the liberties of burghs in general,
the Town Council explained that the burgh of
Edinburgh was the first and most ancient of all
the burghs in the Kingdom, erected many ages ago ;
and by all their old and late evidents the harbour
of Leith did belong to them properly as a part of
the liberty of their burgh, held therewith in free
burgage long before there was any village in that
place ; and by occasion of the erection of the said
port the Lairds of Restalrig and their tenants for
their private use and advantage built the said village,
as near the harbour as they could, upon the utmost
limits of their barony. The city of Edinburgh had
constantly, both before and after they acquired the
village of Leith, their own bailie and his court for
preserving order and doing justice within the bounds

of the harbour, commonly known as the Water Bailie of Leith.

The city of Edinburgh expressly had, by their infeftments and by their Golden Charter, the sole trade of merchandise pertaining to a free burgh royal within the whole bounds of the shire of Edinburgh, and particularly from Edgebuckling Brae on the east, the water of Almond on the west, so far as the shire extends to on the south, and to the midst of the Water of Forth on the north ; so that no trade could be driven by any inhabitant of Leith or by any other not being burgesses of Edinburgh within the village of Leith or in any other part within the shire.

The city of Edinburgh, as often as they found any unfreemen dwelling in Leith encroaching upon their liberties, by exercising the trade of merchandise or otherwise transgressing their rights, have at all times called them to question and have obtained decreets decerning them to desist, and to find caution for that effect.

" His Highness the Lord Protector and his Council of State were pleased by a special Order of the 15th October 1653 to establish the city of Edinburgh in her right of Leith and that the inhabitants (the soldiers only excepted) should be liable to the courts of the magistrates of Edinburgh, as heretofore in civil affairs.

" This being premised with respect to the Royal Burghs in general, and the Burgh of Edinburgh in particular, the magistrates and council did represent the sadness of their condition these years past, and how calmly they had suffered the want of their estates, commodities and liberties pertaining to their port and village of Leith, and how the said liberties had been encroached upon by both natives and foreigners, which they did the more patiently endure considering the great and weighty affairs of the Commonwealth: and that although they were restored to their said rights and liberties, yet they were still troubled by a number of the inhabitants of Leith, against whom the magistrates of Edinburgh intending to make application for redress they by way of prevention to colour their injuries had presented that Petition to his Highness, full of untruths, calumnies, reflections, and every way seditious, and liable to the punishment expressed in King James the Fifth his 4th Parliament Ch. 26, whereby it is statute, that such as troubled or molested the magistrates of burghs or merchants thereof in using their liberties and privileges granted to them by the Kings of Scotland might be accused criminally as common oppressors: And that the said Petition might the better appear to be such, the said magistrates and council of Edinburgh did make particular Answers thereto, as follows "—

(1) They denied that the inhabitants of Leith had ever enjoyed the liberty of choosing their own magistrates, but on the contrary this right belonged to Edinburgh since they had acquired the superiority of the said village; and when Leith had belonged to the Laird of Restalrig, he and not the inhabitants had always appointed a baron bailie for the barony; and nowhere in Scotland had villages any power to

choose their own magistrates without a special right from the overlord.

(2) They denied having laid any arbitrary or unlimited taxes upon lands and houses in Leith, but referred to the monthly assessment imposed by Cromwell upon all Scotland, a due proportion of which was laid upon Leith.

(3) With respect to the mark upon each tun of goods imported, this had been granted by the late King, but such was their respect to the English that they discharged the uplifting thereof from their goods coming from England, being native commodities, and had given orders to exact the same only from outlandish goods; but the English had refused to pay the said duty altogether even on goods coming from France and other countries beyond the seas.

(4) With respect to those who were forced to leave their houses in Leith and dwell in Edinburgh, the town of Edinburgh had just reason not to suffer any to dwell and exercise trade in Leith, "yet the gentlemen of the English nation now dwelling there and those of the garrison knew very well the Magistrates did offer to dispense with a great part of their liberty in their favours."

(5) With respect to the refusal to allow goods brought into the port to be sold until they were proffered to the Town Council, the continual custom here had been that "where any strangers or unfreemen not being burgesses of the burgh brought goods to the port thereof they are holden to make offer; and yet since the year 1650 no such offer had been made to the Council of Edinburgh by the petitioners."

Cromwell and Leith

(6) The complaint about the beam or weighhouse was groundless and unreasonable for it had been the city's right in all ages and by charters from the most ancient kings to have a public beam or weighhouse; and for the ease of the people of the port they had caused settle a weighhouse in Leith that the merchants and others might be free from the trouble of coming to Edinburgh.

(7) It was the town of Edinburgh's unquestionable liberty not to suffer any to sell wine or beer, make malt or brew for sale, but such as Edinburgh authorised in Leith; if it were otherwise by the confusion and number of taverns and tap-houses there would be nothing but debauch and vices. The Magistrates had settled that there should be twenty-six vintners only in Leith, and for their liberty to trade they paid an acknowledgment to the city; but now neither was their number limited nor had any duty been exacted that the garrison of Leith might be the better served; nor had they lifted any taxes upon wine or tobacco more than from their own burgesses; "yet such had been their tenderness and respect to the garrison at Leith that they had not exacted from the inhabitants these dues as they might have done, still using their best endeavours to settle all questions betwixt the garrison and them in love and peace."

(8) With respect to the ballast and other dues, formerly the masters of ships had been forced to call on the "raskally multitude" of women to carry sand and ballast; but the Magistrates had provided public boats and servants for this purpose at an easier rate than in many ports of England, France

or Holland, and all the dues were not able to pay the expense of the harbour, pier, and bridge.

(9) As for the gift of excise upon ale and beer, the town of Edinburgh owed the Lord Protector great thanks, for it had saved them from utter ruin and no more was exacted in Leith than in Edinburgh; and as to markets, Leith wanted none they ever had, both flesh market and bread market; and as to a meal market, Edinburgh had willingly, for the benefit of the garrison, upon their own expenses, erected a meal market which was near finished.

(10) As to the cess, the collecting thereof was interrupted by the coming in of the English army, and as occasion offered the collector demanded payment of the arrears long ago advanced by Edinburgh for Leith. As to the quartering of soldiers and "billgates," Edinburgh was never debtor since it was done by authority of the officers of the army. As to the bailies of Leith, the water bailie's fee was only £8 sterling and a noble; and the other bailie £4 sterling and 10 groats; which was not answerable to the meanest part of their charge and labour. It was an unjust charge that Edinburgh collected money in Leith to maintain their agents in England to keep up oppression upon them, for any agents in England (especially their town clerk, Sir William Thomson) were maintained by their own expense and for their own necessary affairs. As to the paving of the streets, the city having from ancient times right to the public roads which lead to and from the port, were willing to be at the charge of mending them; but as to private lanes and passages it was reasonable that each heritor should be at the

charge thereof before his own doors, as was the custom in all towns and villages.

(11) As to those of the English nation in Leith, the Magistrates were sorry that those to whom their laws, customs, and privileges were unknown, should have so rashly joined in that unreasonable and scandalous petition. As to those of the Scots nation it was over-boldness in them, and they deserved to be censured as calumniators and seditious persons who thus charge their Magistrates and superiors, whom God, lawful authority, and just rights had placed over them; "as if all law did not allow the exercise of just power and liberties and subordination of people to Magistrates and superiors; or as if all men promiscuously should have the liberty of merchandising and trafficking; and have the power of choosing their own Magistrates."

"In respect whereof it was humbly desired that the judges might be pleased to look upon those of the petitioners of the Scots nation living under Edinburgh jurisdiction as scandalous and seditious persons; and that the judges might report to His Highness the Lord Protector their just Answers and defences, from whose goodness and justice the Magistrates were confident to be protected in their rights, freedoms, and privileges, and for whose happy government they should ever pray."

The Edinburgh Answers were delivered to General Monk on 26th September 1655, and copies Replies and were also given to Judges Smith and Duplies. Swinton, who were associated with Monk; and a copy was lodged for the men of Leith. It does not appear that Monk and the

104

Judges ever brought the parties before them, but in the old-fashioned way of pleading, one paper led to another in a long series. Hence there were Replies, Duplies, Triplies and Quadruplies on either side, each of these documents answering another and repeating the previous arguments. The following passages occur in the papers for Leith :—

The people of Leith had reason to regard with envy the rich and flourishing condition of Edinburgh, which, because of its courts and colleges and schools was a place of repair for the whole country, and might be abundantly upheld and maintained in all ages without the necessity of enslaving neighbour towns, or by monopolising within its walls the whole trade of Scotland. Leith desired to have the common use and liberty of the harbour as given to other free burghs for payment of the ordinary dues on ships. The water bailie should have no jurisdiction over the people of the port, but his proper office was to collect the shore dues, receive ships at their entry, to see their incomings and outgoings timeously managed, the channel cleared and kept navigable, and the failings of the harbour, pier, and shore mended and repaired. As to the impositions on Leith, it was remarkable through the whole Answers of Edinburgh, that "when the inhabitants of Leith complained of the burdens with which they were borne down, their constant answer was that they were used no worse than their own burgesses; and when they claimed any privilege or immunity, then their answer was they could pretend no interest thereto, and by these distinctions they were deprived of all benefit and yet burdened with all taxes." The Golden Charter of 1603, upon which Edinburgh relied, was justly named since "the gold of Edinburgh had procured it from King James at his first going to England, when he was prone to satisfy any Scots desire, especially of so potent and importunate a suitor as the town of Edinburgh ; but this charter extended the liberties of Edinburgh to such vast bounds and was of such a length that the truth thereof was never known to the King." The freedom of Leith would promote trade, and tend to the increase of shipping and the general benefit, nor could there arise therefrom any confusion or prejudice, but both towns would peaceably and separately enjoy the like rights and privileges.

The Edinburgh papers stated the issue as meaning : "Whether Edinburgh which has stood these many hundred years the chiefest and mother of all free burghs in Scotland should be destroyed and ruined to satisfy the covetous desire of a few inhabitants of Leith." The erection of Leith into a free burgh would be an encouragement to all the neighbouring villages of the royal burghs of Scotland to crave the same privileges. "The inhabitants of Leith had the use of the harbour as freely as any unfree men in Scotland, but no inhabitant of Leith nor of any other place without a burgh royal, could exerce any trade or merchandise, outward or inward, and therefore what use the people of Leith were to make of the said harbour must be such as was common to all unfree men and not such as pertained to burgesses of royal burghs. . . . The whole multitude of the people might pretend or desire to have the privileges of the royal burghs called down and destroyed which could bring nothing but confusion and destruction.

"It is evident that the town of Edinburgh has been anciently erected on account of the conveniency of trade and situation at so small a distance from the sea, upon which consideration the port and harbour at Leith were united to the burgh of Edinburgh, and in consideration of the liberties and privileges of the burgesses and citizens of Edinburgh and especially the liberty of traffic at the said place, the town of Edinburgh has been peopled from time to time with burgesses and they have been encouraged to bestow their stocks upon public and private buildings not only for their own accommodation but in effect for the whole kingdom, the said town having always been the metropolis and seat of the supreme judicatories, which they did upon public confidence, that their liberties should neither be taken from them nor undermined. This then being the case and it being undeniable that in places adjoining to a seaport, the life and soul of burghs and cities is the liberty of trade, which cannot animate two bodies and towns at so near a distance, but of necessity the erecting of the one would be the destroying of the other; *et ortus unius interitus alterius* it follows consequently that Leith cannot be erected into a Royal Burgh upon the pretence of the conveniency of trade at the foresaid port without undermining and undoing Edinburgh and the liberties thereof."

Cromwell and Leith

As the controversy developed the arguments were repeated with increasing emphasis, especially on the part of Edinburgh, but the parties were led to concentrate on what was really the crux of the matter, namely the acquisition by the city of Edinburgh of the superiority of Leith in 1565. The transactions on this head had begun ten years earlier by a contract entered into between the Dowager Queen Mary of Lorraine and the inhabitants of Leith, whereby the former obliged herself to purchase and procure from Logan of Restalrig the superiority of Leith for the sum of £3000 as the price thereof; and also obliged herself to procure the said burgh erected into a royal burgh. Logan accordingly conveyed the superiority to the Queen and received payment of the price mentioned, so that the whole terms of the arrangement had been performed by the people of Leith. The Queen Dowager had further granted a Commission of Bailliary to several of the inhabitants of Leith "to endure ay and while the said town of Leith was erected into a royal burgh or at least until the sum advanced by them in purchasing the right of superiority was paid back"; conform to which several persons had been chosen bailies by the inhabitants of Leith. The arrangement left it to Queen Mary to give or to withhold consent to the erection of Leith, but however desirous to complete the transaction, she had in fact been driven by her necessities to bargain away the superiority to Edinburgh, and was never in a position to repay the unfortunate people of Leith who had thus spent their money to no purpose. Edinburgh deprecated the discussion of events ninety years old and pointed to her infeftment and possession of the superiority, commenting that any claim competent to Leith "was personal against Queen Mary and was long ago prescribed." The gift of bailliary was described as personal to certain individuals "who became the Queen's bailies and had jurisdiction granted to them over Leith, and it was a wild chimera that the inhabitants should become their own superiors because there was no infeftment and no land in Scotland was allodial." This passage of local history is well known and therefore need not be pursued further.

The documents referred to were all given in during the year 1655, and after some delay, which will be explained shortly, there was **The Decision.** issued on 31st July 1656, an "Act of Cromwell's Council in Scotland concerning the superiority of Leith." This Act refers to the papers of parties which had been received by General Monk, who had called the two Judges to consider the same; but they "had no time" to consider the case which was therefore by Cromwell's order referred to his Council in Scotland. The Council having seriously considered the petition and writs and papers, "found and declared that the superiority of and over Leith is of right vested in

the city and corporation of Edinburgh; . . . and
that the said inhabitants of Leith have no right of
jurisdiction and chusing of their own Magistrates
within the said village; and therefore that their
desire to be incorporated should not be granted, as
being contrary to the rights and liberties of the
city of Edinburgh and inconsistent with justice."

When the people of Leith had recovered from
this disappointing blow they perhaps called to mind
the proverb which warns ordinary men against putting
their faith in princes; "the worldly hope men set
their hearts upon turns ashes." History had indeed
repeated itself with General Monk taking the place of
Mary of Lorraine. The decision has been denounced
by Leith historians, and certainly it was not free
from suspicious circumstances. It seems odd that
the Judges "had no time" to consider the case, and
that the decision was delayed until Edinburgh had
provided the money required for building the Citadel.
The following passage taken from *Nicoll's Diary*
gives the accepted explanation: "The Protector
and Counsall of England with his Heyness counsell
sittand heir at Edinburgh for the government thairof
haiffing intentioun to beg a citadaill on the north
syde of the brig of Leith they delt with the toun
of Edinburgh ather to big that citadaill or ellis to
lois thair libertie and superioritie of Leith. The toun
of Edinburgh not willing to tyne thair superioritie
did agree with the great counsall to advance thrie
scoir thousand pundis scottis twiching the bigging

of the citadaill and so the Inglisches began to cast
the trenches and enter to that work on the north
syde of Leith upon Monday 26 of May 1656."

According to the usual accounts the Citadel in
North Leith was erected by Monk on, or adjacent to,
the site of the church of St Nicholas.
The Citadel.
It was pentagonal in form and faced
with hewn stone; it had five bastions with barracks
and other accommodation; and extended 400 feet
one way and 250 feet the other. The church of
St Nicholas and parts of the Citadel are shown on the
map in Dr Robertson's *Sculptured Stones of Leith.*

In a letter to the Protector dated 11th July 1657
Monk wrote, "he that commands it may keep six
foot water constantly in the moat if he pleases so
that it cannot be undermined and if the enemy should
make a gallery over it he may let in the water and
destroy it at pleasure; . . . and for battery the work
is so thick with stone and clay that there will be no
damage, so that the work will be for your Highness
service in keeping this country in awe and maintaining a footing for your interest here more than
any port in Scotland; and if he be a man that under-
stands his business that commands it in time of
danger, I do not see how any enemy can take it."

John Ray writing in 1661 thus describes it:—
"At Leith we saw one of those citadels built by
the Protector, one of the best fortifications that
ever we beheld, passing fair and sumptuous. There
are three forts advanced above the rest, and two

Cromwell and Leith

platforms; the works round about are faced with freestone towards the ditch and are almost as high as the highest building within; and withal thick and substantial. Below are pleasant, convenient and well-built houses for the governor, officers and soldiers, and for magazines and stores; there is also a capacious chapel, the piazza or void space within is as large as Trinity College in Cambridge great court. The building cost £100,000 stg., indeed I do not see how it could cost less. In England it would have cost more."

The purpose, meantime, is not to give a general account of the Citadel, but to bring together some information on the subject which has been gathered from certain titles and documents in the City Chambers which have been grouped together as "The Rights of the Houses, etc. in North Leith whereon Oliver Cromwell erected the Citadel." Doubtless these writs were handed over on the occasion of the purchase of the property of the Citadel by the Corporation.

It has been stated by certain writers that the Citadel was built on the site of St Nicholas' Church and churchyard; while other writers have stated that Cromwell appropriated the then glebe of North Leith for his purpose. It is odd that the numerous titles in the possession of the Corporation do not throw any light on these statements, which may nevertheless be correct. The titles in question relate to some twenty separate subjects, and indicate that

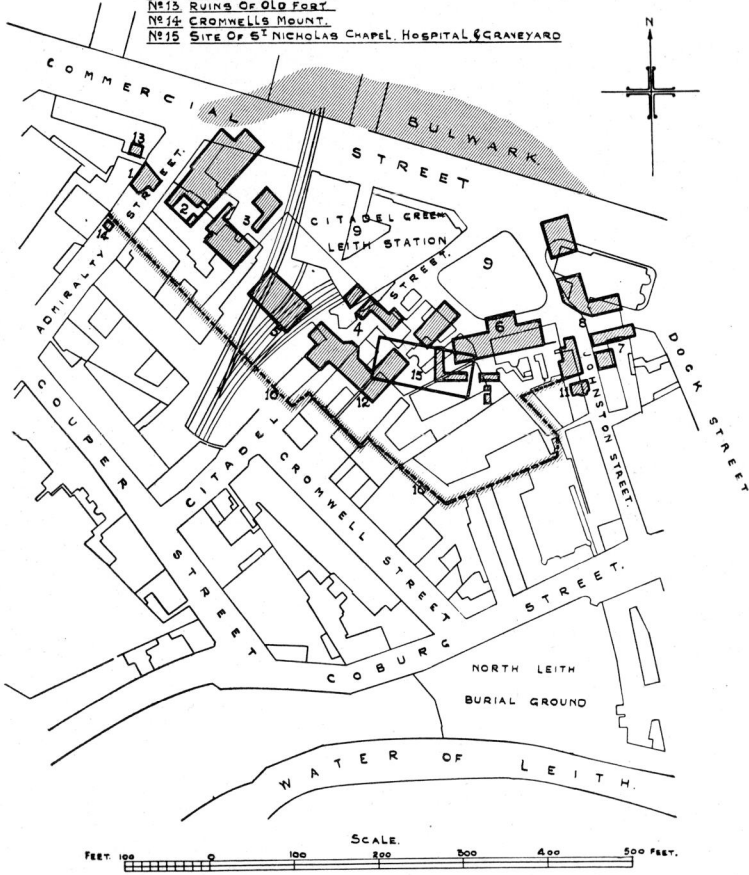

N

COMMERCIAL

BULWARK

STREET

13

ADMIRALTY STREET

2

3

CITADEL GREEN
LEITH STATION

STREET

9

COUPER

STREET

CITADEL

CROMWELL STREET

10

4

6

15

12

8

7

11

JOHNSTON STREET.

DOCK STREET

STREET

16

COBURG STREET.

NORTH LEITH
BURIAL GROUND

WATER OF LEITH.

SCALE.

FEET. 100   0   100   200   300   400   500 FEET.

PLAN OF CITADEL OF LEITH

112

the site of the Citadel was marked off, and the several interests therein were acquired by compulsory purchase, very much in the same way as the Corporation nowadays may take lands required for some public purpose. The several prices are not always given, but the total was not less than £2500 sterling; and the fact that there were at least twenty proprietors indicates that the area was fully developed. Each property was valued and paid for separately, and the transaction was completed by the grant of a disposition in ordinary form in favour of the Lord Protector, and by the delivery of a progress of titles including in some cases writs which date back as far as 1512.

For the purpose of fixing the price to be paid, a "Survey and Valuation or Comprisement" was made by two persons on behalf of the Commonwealth of England, by order and appointment of Lieutenant-Colonel Timothy Wilks, Deputy-Governor of the garrison of Leith. The valuators fixed the yearly value and this was capitalised at eleven years' purchase. In one case, which may be taken by way of example, a certain John Tait, described as a gardener, received £198 sterling as the price of six dwelling-houses belonging to him, part of the lands of Greendykes, for which he granted a Disposition which narrates that the purchase had been made by Lieutenant-Colonel Wilks, " Commissioner appointed by the right honourable General Monk upon the behalf of His Royal Highness the Lord Protector, for purchasing and buying any lands, tenements and ground in North Leith towards the building of a Citadel there." This Disposition was dated 3rd September 1656. The prices varied with the valuations, the highest apparently being £781, which was the amount paid to John Mayne, Mealmaker, for "land and tenements." In one case a sum of £7, 10s. was paid to James Logan of Coustoun in respect of a "ruinous house." In another case a certain property was found to be worth £30 sterling yearly, which at eleven years' purchase extended to £330, and this price was paid to Alexander Kincaid of Hillhousefield in respect of "the great tenement called the manor house of Hillhousefield," bounded by greenyards on the east; by a certain land on the west; by the highway passing from Leith to Bonnytoun on the north; and the Water of Leith on the south.

The boundaries are in most cases too indefinite to be recognised, but the following have been noted : St Ninian's Vennel, the vennel of St Nicholas; the common highway, or the highway from Leith to Bonnington corresponding apparently with the modern Coburg Street; the Water of Leith called the Reach; the green on the north part, and the Links of North Leith, which apparently extended from the Citadel westwards over an area now partly covered by the old West Dock and partly by the sea at the Marine Parade. The property acquired in connection with the Citadel seems to have extended to the Water of Leith over what is now the old churchyard of North Leith; and it included a roadway or passage leading to the Water of Leith along the line of Commercial Street as seems to be indicated on John Rennie's Map of Leith made in 1804.

The subjects purchased were variously described as tenements, houses, shops, a barn, a hall, a great cabbage garden. The parties to the deeds are in some cases vaguely designated as "indwellers"; but the variety of occupations more specifically mentioned seems to indicate the presence here of a considerable community of people, viz. :—masons, tailors, smiths, slaters, timbermen, brewers, sailors, skippers, maltmen. There are also references to the master of a ship called the *James* of Leith; to a Leith merchant in Rouen; and another merchant in "Wadden in Germany."

Certain of the prior Charters and Writs bear to have been granted by the following parties as superiors of the subjects, viz: George Abbot of the Abbacy of Holycross beside Edinburgh (1512); Abbot Robert (1532); Robert, Commendator of the Monastery of Holyroodhouse, and Alexander, Abbot of Cambuskenneth his coadjutor (1542); Adam, Bishop of Orkney and Zetland, Commendator of the Monastery of Holycross near Edinburgh (1575); Robert, Earl of Roxburgh; Sir Ludovick Ballenden of Auchinnoul, Lord Justice Clerk; Sir James Ballenden of Broughton. Other names that occur include the following :—Andrew Wood of

Largo (1598); Thomas and John Kincaid of
Warriestoun; James Crawford of Bonnytoun;
William Rutherford of Sunlaws; Adam Couper,
Clerk of Session, and Sir John Coupar of Gogar:
Thomas Fowlis, Goldsmith; Walter and James
Logan, Clerks of Canongate; David and John
Wauss or Vaus (1562 and 1587). The name of
Vaus or Vans has long persisted in North Leith,
and in the Dock Act of 1807 there is a reference
to the Glebe of North Leith, "commonly called
Vans garden."

One of the dispositions bears to have been granted
in November 1657 by Sir John Towers or Tours of
Inner Leith. This family owned the lands of
Wardie, and it will be recalled that in 1500 the Laird
of Inverleith received license from King James IV.
to build a tower on Wardie Brow to defend his lands
from English invaders. This tower is said to have
occupied the site of the present Wardie House in
Boswall Road; and probably it had been destroyed
in the Hertford invasion, thus failing in the purpose
for which it had been built. For a sum of £60
Sir John Tours conveyed to Cromwell "the mannour
place or house of Wardie," but not the ground on
which it stood; with power to Cromwell to pull
down the house and remove the stones and timber
thereof; and he also granted a tack of the "stone
quarry lying betwixt the house of Wardie and the
sea, so long as they should be abuilding of the
Cittadel, with power to win all manner of stones

therein for the foresaid use; and if they had any use for any whins they were empowered to cut 100 faggots of whins in Wardie Muir and no more."

The Citadel was partly demolished at the Restoration and the site gifted to the Earl of The Charter to Lauderdale, who obtained a charter the City. erecting it into a free burgh of barony. It appears that this was a ruse on his part adopted for the purpose of extorting money out of Edinburgh. Having succeeded in alarming the citizens he offered to sell the property for £6000, and the Magistrates were afraid to incur his displeasure by the offer of a less sum.

In 1663 a Charter under the Great Seal was granted in favour of the town of Edinburgh of the "Cittadel of Leith and pertinents." The grant included the "magazine houses, church and haill other houses, biggings, walls, ditches, wooden and iron works, stones, bounds, lands, precincts, haven and port . . . possessed or acquired by the late usurpers." The Citadel is described as bounded and limited as follows:—"having the Links, commonly called the Links of Newhaven belonging to the burgh of Edinburgh and the sea at the lowest ebbing thereof on the north and west; the westward stone wall of the shore of Leith and the utmost eastward point of the walk or alley leading from the said Cittadel to the said stone wall on the east towards the sea and which alley also belongs to the said Cittadel; All and Whole that great void space belonging to the said Cittadel lying contigue upon the north side of the chief street of North Leith and southwest side of the said Cittadel . . . and the houses and tenements belonging to John Hutchison baxter in North Leith and the biggings pertaining to (blank) and the said great void space as it is limited on the east by the Water of Leith . . . and also that piece of waste ground belonging to the said Cittadel lying discontigue from the Cittadel on the south side of the chief street of North Leith bounded betwixt the lands of William Somerville, seaman on the west, the houses or tenements of John Gray on the east, the water of Leith on the south and the chief street of North Leith on the north parts."

The property thus acquired was feued out in lots and at different times by the Corporation. From certain plans in the City Chambers and from an examination of the titles granted to vassals it has been possible to construct a map of the Citadel showing the various buildings therein, which have been identified to correspond with old descriptions as far as this can now be done. Thus the Gunners' House was "bounded between the drawbridge or port on the north; the ditch on the east, the passage to the drawwell on the south and the common way or vennel on the west." The Old Guard Hall was bounded "between the canal towards the port or entry to the said Citadel on the east; and the public road leading to the said Citadel on the north." The house called Charlotte Hall with pertinents was bounded on the north by Dock or Commercial Street, and on the east by ground feued to the Railway Company. In a conveyance granted to the Railway Company in 1898 of "Cromwell's Barracks," it is stated that the Railway Company were to have all the barrack houses except the west stairs thereof and a small angle near the subjects called Charlotte Hall. These barrack stairs were removed in recent years.

In the year 1666 a Petition was presented to the Corporation by Mr James Reid, Minister of North Leith, bearing that the Glebe of that church had been taken away by the Citadel of Leith and craving that the Council would be pleased to make up the same. The Council out of favour to the petitioner instructed the Water Bailie of Leith and the Baron Bailie of the Canongate to cause measure off so much land as would correspond to the former glebe to form a glebe in all time coming for the ministers serving the cure of North Leith. The area of the glebe thus granted is indefinite, but it appears that it was bounded on the west by ground formerly possessed by Thomas Peacock, tacksman of the Links of Newhaven; and on the south by the high road leading from North Leith to Newhaven now called Couper Street and partly by ground belonging to Peter Couper, carter in Leith, and others; by lands and hedges on the east; and partly by the seashore on the north. It lay outwith the area of the Citadel.

The parishioners of North Leith, having been

deprived of their burial-ground at the old church of St Nicholas, were allowed for a time to bury their dead in the churchyard of South Leith. In the year 1664, however, the Town Council of Edinburgh gave them a piece of garden ground on the south side of their ancient cemetery, part of the area which had been acquired by Cromwell; and this small space continued to be the only burial-ground in North Leith for about 200 years.

In John Russell's book, *The Story of Leith*, a picture is given of Cromwell's House in the Citadel, which it seems certain that Cromwell never saw. During the eighteenth century the Citadel became a fashionable suburb and a quarter for aristocratic residents, these including the Duke of Gordon, Lady Bruce, Sir William Erskine, and Lady Eleanor Dundas. The South Leith Records under date 27th August 1719 refer to a payment of 100 merks received by the Kirk Treasurer "for the late Laird of Grant his corpse lying in the Session House." This was Alexander who had held Edinburgh Castle against the rebels in 1715 and aided his friend the Duke of Argyle in driving Mackintosh of Borlum from the Citadel. He probably had been with his regiment in Leith and had died at the Citadel.

CHAPTER V

THE office of Town, or, as it was formerly called, Common Clerk of Edinburgh, was an important one. It is therefore the more surprising that the early history of the burgh makes so little mention of these officials. Even the list which can be gathered from the Records, judging from the gaps, is incomplete.

The duties of the office were numerous, although they never seem to have precluded the possibility of the Clerk's carrying on private work as well, a practice which, although it did not prove altogether satisfactory, was continued till the middle of the nineteenth century.

A considerable part of the Common Clerk's time was taken up with his attendance on the meetings of the Town Council and his recording of their proceedings. The other duties were laid down by statutes usually renewed at each appointment. The earliest of these are found in 1579 for Alexander Guthrie, first of that name to hold office. It is provided that the Common Clerk should have two Depute Clerks to be provided and paid by him, one of whom was to be known as the Principal Depute.

Some Town Clerks of Edinburgh

A part of his duty was to sign all acts, decreets, and sasines on behalf of the Town. He was forbidden to do any of these things without an authorisation of the Council. He was responsible for producing all copies of Town acts, titles or writs, for which, if done on behalf of the Council, he could exact no fee, if for other people a statutory fee could be asked. The Common Clerk or a deputy appointed by him had to attend the Convention of Royal Burghs as clerk. He had the charge of the Town lawsuits, which were frequent, but might not initiate actions without the orders of the Provost and Bailies. He had the care of the Burgh Court Books and was bound to produce them when required; this was necessary because there was a tax of 12d. in the pound payable by everyone who lost an action brought before the Provost and Bailies, the money going to the poor of the Town. The Clerk was responsible also for keeping a rent-roll of the Town lands and a Book of Acts and Statutes regarding such of the Town's rights as the freighting of ships, the making of burgesses, the judging of neighbourhood cases and the convening of Council, besides the ordinary statutes of the burgh. The oath taken by the Clerks on assuming office was recorded among other directions. By it they swore obedience to the King, the Provost, Bailies, Council, Deacons and community of Edinburgh, promised faithful service "without feid or favour of ony persoun," not to give advice hurtful to the common weal, to obey all orders made or to be made, to give good counsel and inform the Council of all laws and statutes affecting the welfare of the burgh.

The office was not one which carried a salary, for the Clerk, like the other officials of the Town, received only the gift of a burgess-ship yearly. But the fees connected with his duties to the public made the office a sufficiently lucrative one, and so late as the beginning of the nineteenth century it was considered worth a purchase price of £1400.

A revised table of fees made in 1608 shows that there were forty-eight pieces of work which could be done for the public at fees varying from one shilling to four pounds Scots. These included copies of proceedings in all cases tried before the Burgh Court, charters, contracts, charter-parties the booking of apprentices and the issue of guild tickets. The scale was subjected to tolerably frequent revision, always with a tendency to increase the amount to be paid.

The Common Clerkship was in the gift of the Town Council, but it appears, for a time at least, that the Clerks possessed influence in the nomination of their successors, for the first Alexander Guthrie, appointed in 1579, was followed by his son and his grandson, both of the same name, their period of office covering ninety-two years.

After the appointment of the third Alexander

Some Town Clerks of Edinburgh

Guthrie, which was possibly the natural recognition of the services of his two predecessors, the history of the Clerkship is given in much greater detail. There appears to have been much trouble over different appointments, due probably to the way in which these were made. These seem to have become a reward for political services, or even in some cases pure favouritism, and the practice became prevalent of letting the Deputes do the work, while the Common Clerks took on duties not originally part of the office. Mr John Hay, when he became Clerk, was the first to be employed in such duties, being sent to England for long periods to look after the interests of the Burgh at Court. This was a change necessitated by the departure of James VI., and one which proved troublesome and expensive to the Council by reason of the long delays involved in getting business done.

In 1618 the second Alexander Guthrie resigned office in favour of his son, third of the name, after a tenure of forty-eight years, and the latter and Mr John Hay were appointed conjunct Clerks.

The next mention of the Clerks was in 1622, when an Act of the Court of Session exempted them as notaries from having all their protocol books signed by the Lord Clerk Register, as was the practice for notaries of other places. The reason given for this favour was that the inconveniences due to dishonest notaries had been prevented by

Appointments

the Magistrates of the Burgh, who had appointed such "famous, honest and unsuspect persons" that no abuses need be feared. Thereafter only the first protocols after appointment were to be so signed.

In March 1624 William Hay, son of Mr John Hay, Common Clerk and apparently also Commissary Clerk of Edinburgh, was admitted as deputy in his father's absence. Ten years later, upon the promotion of the latter to the office of Lord Clerk Register as Sir John Hay of Baro, Kt., William Hay was made depute in the absence of Alexander Guthrie at Court. The appointment was confirmed in 1634 during the prolonged absence of Guthrie, employed in various affairs of the Burghs of Scotland. The Common Clerk seems to have been sent frequently on such business, for again, in 1637, Hay acted as Clerk when Guthrie was attending the Convention of Royal Burghs "in the commoun effayres of this kingdome." Apparently the appointment was never made a definite one, for in 1646 a new gift of the Clerkship was made to Mr Alexander Guthrie and William Thomson, and to the survivor of the two.

In 1648 there is one of the rare mentions of political matters in the Records, when the Council solemnly disclaimed the action of their predecessors in approving the Engagement. This was the treaty by the Earls of Loudon, Lanark and Lauderdale with Charles I., by which he, though refusing to sign or enforce the Covenant, promised to establish

Presbyterianism in England for three years, in exchange for which he was to have the Scots army at his disposal. The Kirk opposed the Engagement, and the Town Council of that date sided with them. They enforced the order of the Committee of Estates requiring the removal from office of any who had been accessory to the treaty. Among these was William Thomson, who accordingly was dismissed, in spite of his petition that his case might be left to the Committee of Estates. He undoubtedly had committed himself by " framing and writing the acts of council and by writing and subscryving of the bands for the forty thousand pound paid in name of the Toun to the General Commissar for their levy to the last unlawful engagement and that notwithstanding the declarations of the kirk and the petitions of the six kirk sessions given in to prevent that guiltiness," but it might be questioned whether he, as Clerk, was the person primarily responsible in the matter. But the Council evidently required a scapegoat and declared him incapable of holding office again. They at the same time confirmed Alexander Guthrie in all his rights, including the payment of 2000 merks yearly, as paid formerly to him by Thomson for his share of the office. The new conjunct Clerk was Mr Andrew Ker, Clerk to the General Assembly, who seems to have been reluctant to accept office, for he hesitated till November 1648, and upon his acceptance the Council signed the deed of gift.

Vacancies

An Act of Council, a year later, authorised the payment of £600, 11s. 8d. to their dismissed Clerk for repairs done by him to the Clerk's chamber on the north side of St Giles. That place, always inadequate at the best, had been enlarged by taking in the aisle adjoining on the west in 1624, but it seemed to require constant repair without ever being made completely satisfactory.

It is difficult to estimate Thomson's political opinions, if indeed he had any, from the Records, for in February 1651, upon a warrant from the Parliament of the Commonwealth of England ordering the choice of two persons "well affected to the welfare and peace of the Island," the Council elected William Thomson and James Fairbairne commissioners for the burgh, to wait upon the Lord Commissioners at Dalkeith. A few weeks later, after the death of Mr Alexander Guthrie, the Clerkship was declared vacant. Ker was a prisoner in England, and either for that or other reasons the Magistrates thought good not to continue him in office. They recorded a complaint of the piteous state of the burgh through lack of Magistrates, through the burdens on the Common Good, ruined by the troubles, the breaking-up of the Charter House, the disorder of the writs in the Clerk's chamber and the confusion of the Bailie Court Books, due to the absence of Ker. "Taking into consideration the present estate and condition quherin this burgh with all the liberties thereof stands with the English, being now by God's providence reducit under their obedience so that no Magistrate, Counsell nor Government is nor can be heir bot their expres licence and good will," the Council found necessary to choose an able Common Clerk, a post which could not, as they then considered, be filled by Mr Andrew Ker, Clerk to the General and Synodal Assemblies. They therefore dismissed him and appointed William Thomson of Newmylnes as sole Common Clerk. What pressure was put upon them cannot be judged, but it is curious, to say the least, to find the man dismissed four years previously for favouring the Royalists, now become a *persona grata* with the Commonwealth.

Still he must have enjoyed the confidence of the ruling powers, for in July of the same year Thomson was sent as agent in the Town's affairs to London, and the gift of the Clerkship was registered in the Acts of Council. In view of their previous strictures on him, it is remarkable enough to read their opinion of his "good, constant, and sincere affection to their service." Thomson was much absent on different errands, and his servant, Andrew Butter, was admitted as his depute to carry on necessary work in his master's absence. Complete confidence was reposed in the Clerk, and the Council were careful to supply him with the funds requisite for his mission. He cannot have long returned from London when he was again despatched there in October of the same year. The Council charged a committee to draw up his instructions, and, realising that his expenses probably would be great, ordered the Treasurer and collectors to advance to him all the money they had in hand upon his receipt. The Treasurer also was charged to honour any bills of exchange which Thomson might draw upon him in London. This course the Clerk found to be necessary, and in 1654 a demand for £200 sterling found the Treasurer with no money and compelled to borrow at 5 per cent. There is no detailed account of his spendings, but during an absence of eighteen months in London, Thomson received £1283, 11s. 5d. and exceeded that amount by £33, 2s., which was repaid him. In addition to these sums the Council granted him a gratuity of 10,000 merks for the following services to the Town : the recovery of a considerable part of the liberties of Leith, the relief of Heriot's Hospital from sequestration, and the obtaining of the gift of 4d. on the pint of ale and beer for three years and seven months toward the relief of the Town debts.

In all these negotiations Thomson had a free hand, as is evidenced by an Act of the 24th October 1655, which recounts how four blanks, signed by the Provost and Council, had been entrusted to him and Andrew Ramsay, later the notorious Provost, for their use in London. These had not proved to be necessary and subsequently were cancelled. Later in that year he was charged with the supervision of various processes between the Town and Leith and of matters relating to taxation, and the Council marked the favour in which they held him by the gift of a burgess-ship to one of his servants.

Affairs other than those of the Town were entrusted to this Clerk. In 1657, by virtue of a commission from the Protector, he and some others were deputed to take order with the salmon fishings at Berwick. This was sanctioned by the Magistrates, who doubtless had little choice in the matter, in an Act of Council which made mention that his other employments kept him from attending to the work of his office and necessitated the appointment of another Depute Clerk. The choice for this post fell upon another of his servants.

Meanwhile, and not unnaturally, the Clerk's chamber and the papers fell into great disorder. A committee was appointed in 1659 to investigate their condition, who, after an examination delayed for five months, reported that the Town's manuscripts had "become rotten in the present Clerk's chamber in respect of the unwholesome air thereof, not having a chimney therein." Rooms were therefore allotted for them above the Council House for their preservation, a place presumably in the south-west corner of St Giles.

In February 1660 Thomson was despatched again to London to seek a means of relief for the Town's burden of debt. A month later he wrote desiring to be recalled or to be given permission to return at his discretion, when he should find that he was doing no good. It appears that he had other business on hand, for the Council summoned a meeting of the four Burghs to discuss the request. Possibly it was the political situation which made his presence in London necessary, for in the beginning of May the Clerk, who apparently had not been recalled, wrote concerning a draft for £300 sterling and informed the Council that he was going to Holland to see the King. Such a step could not have been taken by him without instructions, and the letter which the Magistrates ordered to be written for presentation to Charles II. seems to indicate what the business was that kept him in the south.

The Magistrates shared the popular desire for the restoration of the King, and their letter expressed in the warmest terms the Town's loyalty to Charles II. It did not omit to record the afflictions under which they had laboured during the late government, in which, however, they had acquiesced. A letter from Thomson of the 20th May 1660, dated at Breda, proves that he was the envoy of the Scottish Burghs to the King, and had offered on their behalf the assurance of their loyalty and "a poore myte of £1000 sterling as a token of their love and respects." The Clerk appears to have been charmed with his reception, for, after being careful to state that he was no flatterer, he extolled "the mirrour of princes for pietie, knowledge, mercie etc." It is doubtful whether the subject of such praises would have recognised himself in this guise. A committee was appointed on the 6th June to consider the answer to be given to a later letter, the sending of commissioners to London and the manner of paying their Clerk's expenses, the money for which they finally contrived to borrow from the merchants and deacons of crafts.

On the 13th July the Council did not meet, owing to the arrest of the Provost, Sir James Stewart, and his imprisonment in the Castle upon a warrant from the King. A discussion of the situation by certain of the Council and the ministers resulted in a letter to Thomson to inquire the reasons for the arrest, and to ask advice as to how they should act. The Presbytery also required his assistance in the election of a minister to fill a vacancy.

The Magistrates received, on the 7th August, the Royal Warrant for the convening of the Committee of Estates, together with instructions from the Clerk to prepare the Inner House of the Tolbooth in the customary manner. He confessed he did not know in what way this should be done, but left the preparations in the charge of the Council. A few days later other letters were received concerning the Provost, the new officers of State, and the question of a house for the Lord Chancellor, the Earl of Glencairn.

Meanwhile Thomson remained in London, and instructions were sent to him to delay the new impost on ale. He returned in the beginning of November, apparently in favour at Court, as in a Minute of that date it appeared that he had been

knighted. The entry recorded a formal report of his
diligence in the Council's service since his departure
in February. The Magistrates approved his services
and returned him thanks, appointing also a committee to discuss his expenses and the quickest way
of repayment. In the same month they desired
him to inform the Committee of Estates that they
could not be tacksmen of excise either for the burgh
or for the shire. On the 21st December Sir William
Thomson was appointed to meet the King's Commissioner, the Earl of Middleton, at Berwick, and
to warn the Council betimes of his approach.

Sir William seems to have been the first of the
Clerks to combine offices in the Council's gift with
that of Common Clerk, a practice which led to a
continued neglect of official duties. In April 1661
he held the post of collector of the impost on ale,
beer, and wine, and as a consequence was charged
with the administration of the money collected for
the payment of debts due so far back as 1652. In
August of the same year the Council appointed
Sir William Clerk of Leith in addition to his office
as Common Clerk. He was to hold the office for
life, but the reservation was made that this should
be no precedent to any Principal Clerk of Edinburgh
to claim it in future. A Depute Clerk was appointed
by Thomson to do the work and a committee
nominated to revise the charges to be exacted
by him.

A month later he reported to the Council his

proceedings with the brewers of Edinburgh, Leith, and Portsburgh. The Council commended his diligence and invited him to continue, in order to obtain the farming of the imposition on ale and beer. Shortly after he was granted powers to imprison all who refused to pay the tax.

About three years later, in 1664, Sir William fell into disfavour with the Council, and was accused of neglect of his duty in not causing the tacksmen of the imposition to sign the tack already signed by the Magistrates, "which they conceaved to be ane high affront and abuse done to the Counsell." The Clerk apologised, but the Magistrates considered themselves doubly affronted inasmuch as Thomson was Common Clerk and had 6500 merks allowed to him for his work in connection with the imposition. The tack was a matter of great importance to the Town, involving as it did a sum exceeding 80,000 merks, and the Council avenged the neglect by deposing their Clerk from all his offices. The matter did not rest there. The deacons of crafts protested that the deposition was illegal, having been made by a few of the Council, and therefore an infringement of their rights. Sir William petitioned the Council to no purpose, and finally the matter was brought before the Privy Council. While the case was under their consideration, two servants of the deposed Clerk were deputed to carry on the necessary work, and the deacons again recorded their adherence to their protest.

Dismissal of the Clerk

After the Michaelmas elections the new Council reviewed the affair and Sir William's summons of reduction before the Lords of Session and approved it. The Dean of Guild and deacons of crafts dissented again, on the grounds that the ordinary Council without the extraordinary deacons had not the power to take such a step, and there the matter rested for a year, while it was resolved to make all such employments in future "during the Council's pleasure." After that delay, choice was made of a new Clerk, Mr Thomas Young. The appointment was not an enduring one: Young was in bad health and Depute Clerks were named to carry on the work. He died within three years, and on the 20th August 1668 William Ramsay, son of Sir Alexander Ramsay, Lord Provost, and Mr James Rocheid were appointed conjunct Clerks. The choice of the former must have been a piece of favouritism, for it appears that he was young and had not finished his education. Meanwhile Rocheid carried on the work of the Clerkship.

With characteristic avoidance of unpleasantness, the Records omitted at the time to chronicle the further proceedings on the part of Thomson to obtain reinstatement. That something did occur is shown in 1670, when the conjunct Clerks resigned their office to be re-elected for life, after the Council had passed an Act rescinding all other Acts contrary to that purpose. The Magistrates were forced to admit the claim of Sir William Thomson either to the office or to indemnification for his dismissal, as is shown some years later, and in October 1670 they discussed what sum should be paid to their Clerks in view of the fact that they had no profits after they had paid to Thomson 4000 merks yearly. A committee, named to discuss the affairs of the Clerks, recommended an annual payment to each Clerk of 1000 merks during Sir William's lifetime.

Rocheid must at this time have given attention to the neglected work of the office, for, towards the end of the year, he received £200 sterling for his services in rearranging the Charterhouse.

The absence of one of the Clerks, presumably William Ramsay, during part of 1671 was provided for by the election of two deputes. The length of the absence was about eight months, and the Clerk found it advisable to apologise for his delay in London. The Magistrates, possibly as a consequence, thought good to define the length of the holiday due to the Clerks, which was to correspond with that of the Town Court, during which they might "recreat themselves with the cuntrie or abrod where they think most fitt and convenient."

Mr William Ramsay was formally admitted to office on the 15th October 1673, and at the same time Alexander Hay was appointed Depute Clerk.

The explanation of the Town Council's position with regard to Sir William Thomson found a place in the Records in November of the same year. The

CVRIA Supremj Conventus Ordinum Regni Scotiæ
Vulgo Domus Parliamentj

The Parliament House in Edinborrough by I.G.

THE OLD PARLIAMENT HOUSE

Compensation for Dismissal

Act of Council related and approved the agreement between Thomson and the two Clerks, and gave the story of his appeal to the Privy Council and to the Court of Session. Having raised the question of his dismissal by these appeals, Thomson had made a visit to Court on the same errand. By the mediation of the Commissioner, the Earl of Lauderdale, an agreement was arrived at, by which the Common Clerk, then Mr Thomas Young, was to pay Sir William for the possession of the office, 4000 merks a year for life. The arrangement seems to have been hardly fair to the successive Clerks to whom it applied, penalised for the action of the Town Council, and out of pocket to the extent of 2000 merks a year between them, in spite of the Council's grant of 1000 merks each.

Apparently the whole business of the Clerks was unsettled for a time, for from an Act of Council in December 1673 it would appear that Mr James Rocheid had been dismissed and re-appointed by a Royal Warrant.

The agreement with Thomson was terminated by his death in 1675 and, as a consequence, the Council's payment of 2000 merks was revoked. Mr William Ramsay petitioned to be allowed to go abroad for three years to continue his studies, a request which was granted, and his place again filled by Hay as Depute Clerk. Rocheid was absent also at that time on Town business, and the Magistrates passed an Act empowering themselves to exercise his functions, a proceeding interpreted as a slight upon him and rescinded shortly after.

The next step of the Town Council with regard to the Clerks is a curious commentary on their treatment of Thomson. It would seem that they had recognised some irregularity in their treatment of his case, for in 1678 they passed an Act in protection of the Common Clerks, present and to come, to ensure to them a fair and legal trial if they should happen to offend in any way. It was statute that any complaint must be presented in full Council after eight days' notice, and a number of conditions were laid down to procure a fair hearing.

In 1680 the condition of the Town's affairs necessitated a mission to the Duke of Lauderdale, Secretary of State for Scotland, at Court, entrusted to Rocheid. His stay was lengthy and he reported no progress till some months had passed. Then a letter of his to the Council brought the news that the imposition on ale and beer had been renewed to the Town for twenty-one years, being a tax of 2d. on the pint of ale and beer brewed and sold in the Town, of 2 merks on the boll of malt, and 2d. on the pint of beer from landward. He implied that some return was expected by the Duke for his assistance, and informed them that he had drawn a bill for £320 stg. upon the Town for his own expenses. These proceedings were approved first by the ordinary Council, then by the extraordinary deacons. Rocheid

Malversation of the Common Good

remained in London some months longer and again made his report, dealing at length with the assistance obtained from Lauderdale. The Council recorded their approval again, and voted a gratuity to the Secretary of State of £6000, to be paid in instalments. They also apologised to Rocheid for not being able to pay him more than £400, in addition to the gift of a piece of plate valued at £50, owing to the state of their finances.

Some three years later common rumour accused Rocheid (then Sir James) of embezzling a large part of the Town's imposition on ale and beer. The Council at this time seem to have been determined not to believe the charge, if it may be called one, and the Provost, George Drummond, summoned three former Provosts, James Currie, Sir William Binning, and Sir James Dick to confute it. At the same time the conjunct Clerks, Sir James Rocheid and James Hamilton, resigned their office to be reappointed for life.

Rumour was persistent in the case of Rocheid, having probably some basis of truth, for the charge came up again in 1684, and he was deposed upon an accusation of malversation of the Common Good. There was some difficulty in bringing him to book, possibly because of the influence he possessed. A letter from the King to the Marquess of Queensberry, transcribed in the Records, refers to a previous one to the Earl of Middleton forbidding any action against the Clerk. But the later letter having removed the embargo, the Council considered the numerous accusations made against Rocheid.

The indictment was lengthy and serious: it included charges of interfering with the elections of Council for his own ends, and planning to remove "the most considerable and substantious burgesses of the Magistracie" by misrepresenting them at Court; neglecting to keep the accounts of the imposition on ale and beer; making an agreement with the Duchess of Lauderdale to declare that he had paid a larger sum than the £6000 for the gift of the imposition in order to procure the balance for himself; taking a tack of the Society Brewery, which, as an official of the town, he might not do, and attempting to take a tack of the Common Good at 4000 merks below its value. Other charges were of having inserted in the Council Register acts which had not been passed by them, and of omitting to enter protests regarding the dilapidation of the Common Good; of arranging that in all stents, taxes and public burdens his own lands were not assessed; of persuading the Council of Heriot's Hospital to set a tack of their mills for 2800 merks less than their value and 800 merks less than the offered price; of leaving blank pages in the Register for his own purposes; of neglecting to keep the Minute Book of Sasines, and of entering no tacks of the Common Good in the Records; of absenting himself from meetings of the Council; of making inexact additions to an Act of Council concerning the election of deacons, and of taking from the charterhouse writs which concerned the nation as a whole, so that they were not forthcoming when required.

The Provost and Council considered this lengthy accusation, found the most of it proved, and dismissed Sir James Rocheid, and presumably Hamilton too. They then proceeded to elect Mr John Richardson, writer, and John Drummond, son of the Provost, conjunct Clerks. The tenure of office of the new Clerks was not undisturbed, for on the 12th December 1685 they were accused of having granted, by their own authority, a gift of the Clerkship of the Canongate to Mr William Syme, in the absence abroad of Mr James Cathcart of Carbieston, Clerk of that place. They were suspended from the exercise of their office, though the Lord Provost protested. This state of affairs lasted for six days, after which the Clerks were reinstated, having furnished a satisfactory explanation of their conduct.

So far as it is possible to judge, the Magistrates and Council seem to have acted without sufficient consideration in the matter of Sir James Rocheid. Motives in this period of the history of the Town were so mixed that it is hardly safe to assume that those of the Council were completely disinterested. Yet, as against that, the powerful influence, which undeniably Rocheid possessed, would be a sufficient inducement to others to find flaws in the accusation which the Council, for its own purposes, accepted on its face value. In any case an inquiry was opened, beginning with a petition sent by the dismissed Clerk to the King, which was handed over to the Council to deal with. A curious situation thus presented itself : the Magistrates were in the difficult position of being judges, accusers, and witnesses at the same time. The proof of the accusation of tampering with the elections was apparently contained in a letter alleged to have been written by Rocheid to the late James Borthwick of Stow. It had passed into the hands of Sir Robert Baird, who asserted that he had given it to Mr John Richardson, one of the new Clerks. The letter for some reason was not forthcoming. A committee appointed to consider the best policy to adopt, recommended a consultation with the Town's assessors. The interlocutor issued by the latter is inserted at length in the Minutes, and gives the impression that they thought most of the charges required further proof before they could give a definite judgment. But it is impossible to say whether the Magistrates had been biased in supporting the accusations or the assessors in making light of it. The proceedings continued till, on the 5th February 1686, Sir James Rocheid was replaced in office. The reinstatement seems to have been complete, for, a month later, Rocheid was sent on a mission to Viscount Melfort, Secretary of State for Scotland, with petitions on behalf of the Town. A decreet of absolvitor in June of the same year in favour of Rocheid closed the matter.

The Clerk's absence in London was prolonged, as apparently it continued till June 1687. Upon a report received from him as to the progress of his business, the questions of the restoration of the summer session and the Town's impost on ale and beer, the Council voted the payment of his expenses. They also inserted in their Minutes a letter from King James II. commending the reinstatement of Sir James and inviting them "to be kind to him for his present and past services." If half the accusations brought against him were true, he stood little in need of such kindnesses, but the Council complied with the Royal hint, and, with one dissentient voice, voted to their Clerk the sum of £1000 sterling in compensation for his sufferings.

Sir James, on his return from London, formally accepted office, and in spite of the gift mentioned, proceeded to complain that the money he had received so far covered little more than half his expenses. Whereupon a further sum of 160 guineas was allowed him.

It might be thought that there were sufficient proofs of the inadvisability of allowing the Clerks to take on other offices, yet Aeneas McLeod, who had been appointed conjunct Clerk in the place of James Hamilton (*passim*), apparently re-appointed during Rocheid's absence, was made clerk to the stent, an appointment which bred trouble in its turn.

Some Town Clerks of Edinburgh

In December an Act of Council permitted the Clerks to take turns in being present at the meetings of Council.

Little is said of the Council's attitude to the coming of the Prince of Orange, but in December 1688 McLeod was sent to London with Viscount Tarbet, Lord Clerk Register, one of the commissioners appointed to "repair there upon accompt of the publict affairs of the kingdom."

During the years immediately following, the history of the burgh is silent as to the Town Clerks. Doubtless there was enough to occupy the Magistrates to the neglect of the supervision of these officials. So perhaps it was a natural consequence that in 1695 the Council again found reason to censure a Clerk. A petition was presented by the Provost, at the desire of the Council, against McLeod, at that time apparently sole Clerk, on the ground of malversations of the Common Good. McLeod at the next meeting of the Council protested against the petition, and the matter appears to have been dropped till the following January. Then, "considering that the Good Town's affairs suffered much by the defects of Aeneas McLeod their clerk," the Magistrates and Council resolved to prosecute. He was dismissed in September, and the Council, "considering that this tyme bygane the toun hes been misserved by their clerks to the great hurt and detriment of the touns affairs," declared that all future Clerks should each year on the 1st January resign their office into the hands of the Provost, Bailies, and Council to be at their disposal. They also bound themselves not to grant the office *ad vitam aut culpam*, under heavy penalties to such as should promote such a gift, and arranged the form of oath to be taken by subsequent Clerks. Shortly after, James Stewart, advocate, and Mr John Murray, brother of Patrick Murray of Livingston, advocate, were chosen as Clerks. They accepted office and took the new oath. The wording is interesting as affording a probable synopsis of all the offences against the Good Town committed by former Clerks and as being a laudable effort to shut the stable door after many steeds had been stolen.

The additional clauses run as follows : " I shall submitt the dues and casualities accrescing to the office of clerkship to the regulation and determination of the Magistrats and Council and their successors, and shall not advocat or suspend the toun council's proceedings, acts or sentences concerning me in my office, and shall not procure or accept from the present Magistrats and Council or their successors of any gift *ad vitam* and contrary to ane act made by the Magistrats and Council of the 4th September 1696 relative hereunto, . . . I shall not informe, solicite or recommend or any way be myself or other, directly or indirectly confer, treat or medle concerning their elections or making of lites for the same of the Magistrats, Council or deacons within this city or Liberties thereof further than what concerns the discharge of my office, and so oft as

Some Town Clerks of Edinburgh

I break any part of this my oath I doe acknowledge the same to be a Cryme meriting deprivatione and lyable to such a penalty to be imposed by the Magistrats as my Cryme shall happen to merit, not exceeding the sume of fyve thousand merks Scots."

But the prosecution of McLeod, the new appointment and the carefully devised oath, proved equally futile as precautions, for on the 6th October McLeod produced a decreet of the Privy Council ordering the Town Council to repossess him in his office. He added insult to injury on this occasion by protesting that he could not be held responsible for any disorder in the Records of the Town or the papers in the Clerk's chamber, "seeing that others had been put in his room."

After this episode McLeod continued to hold the recovered Clerkship alone till August 1699, when he resigned the "just and equal half" of the office, to which the Council elected Mr George Home, son of the Provost, George Home of Kello. A month later he resigned the other half of the post, to which Mr James Stewart was elected, who had been Clerk previously for a short time during McLeod's temporary dismissal.

From this time the history of the Town Clerks becomes less eventful, at least as regards sensational incidents during their tenure of office. For the remainder of the eighteenth century and the nineteenth century till the appointment of Mr (later Sir) James Marwick as sole Town Clerk, the Records are concerned with the changes of Clerks, the sums paid for the privilege of holding the office, and the difficulties connected with the Clerkships of Leith, Portsburgh and the Canongate, and with the practice of the Town Clerks of conducting their private businesses while occupying the public post.   But, as either occasion did not offer or was not taken, of interfering in public affairs as their predecessors had done, their history does not afford the same interest.

CHAPTER VI

THE AMUSEMENTS OF EDINBURGH

IT has been said, and is generally taken for granted, that the Edinburgh of the Reformation was a dreary place, wholly given over to sermons, fasts, and gloom. The conclusions to be drawn from the Records of the Burgh and from other sources tend to discredit, at least in part, that idea. The Kirk did not think so in 1592, for it found reason to condemn " the great dishonour done to God, speciallie in his holie Sabboth, by a great number of this citie in tyme of divine worship, partlie in ale houses, partlie at profane games in back sides, partlie in opin streets . . . " which they proposed to cure by the division of the town into eight parishes, presumably to give better possibilities of supervision. Some four years later the General Assembly found it necessary to censure their ministers for lightness in behaviour, " gorgeous and light apparrell, in speeche, in using light and profane companie, unlawfull gaiming, as dancing, cairding, dycing and such like," and if the ministers were such, how much more the populace. It was at the same time that they reproved His Majesty James VI., as " blotted with

The West Bow

banning and swearing," for which, his provocations
being considered, it is hard to blame him overmuch,
and the Queen, Anne of Denmark, for her "balling,
nightwaking and sicklyke concerning her gentle-
women."

The explanation of this wholesale condemnation,
which may serve as partial proof that the good town
had its amusements, seems to be that the country had
not yet abandoned completely the practices common
and even commended before the Reformation. For
it is hard to see, when men worked from dawn to
dusk in winter, and sometimes even by candle-light,
and a solid eleven hours in summer, what time they had
for amusement and exercise except on Sundays and
feast days. Feast days the Reformation abolished
and only Sunday was left. What wonder was there
that the ministers had cause to mourn the "profanation of the Sabboth . . . in worldlie turnes, exercising
all kind of wantoun games, keeping of mercats,
dancing, drinking and siclyke." Whatever modern
opinions may be, it is certain that the ordinary
working man, whether lawyer, merchant, craftsman
or labourer had a problem to solve with regard to
finding leisure for amusement.

Therefore it is not surprising to find that much
is learned about the amusements of our forefathers
by the negative way of what they were forbidden
to do at certain times and seasons. A proclamation
by the Magistrates in 1592 is useful as showing both
what the Reformers wished to make the Sunday of

The Amusements of Edinburgh

the Edinburgh folk and what games they played on that day. It runs as follows :—

"Ordanis proclamatioun to be made throw this burgh that, seing the Sabboth day being the Lordis day, it becumis everie Cristiane to dedicate himselff, his houshald and famelie to the service and worschip of God in hering the word, meditating thairupoun and reding the sam, instructing thair fameleis and otherwayis in the exercise of prayer; thairfor commanding and chargeing in our Soverane lordis name and in name of the provest, baillies and counsell of this burgh that na inhabitants of the samyn be themselffis, thair children, servands of fameleis be sene at ony pastymes or gammis within or without the toun upoun the Sabboth day, sic as golf, archerie, rowbowlis, penny stane, kaichpullis or sic uther pastymes . . . and als that thair dochters and wemen servandis be nocht fund playing at the ball nor singing profane sangs upoun the sam day, under sic paynes as the magestratts sall lay to thair charge."

Apparently the inhabitants of Edinburgh had a tolerable choice of amusements. There is no reference available as to where they played golf near the town, but possibly our forefathers were not so particular as their descendants in choosing their courses and found that any open space would do. National game though it be, it is a sad fact that the balls used were imported and paid customs of 3 li. on each dozen.

It is curious to find archery as an amusement, for at one time it was part of the military training of the people, a matter so serious that golf and football had to be forbidden in order that suitable attention might be given to practice. Perhaps, with the increasing use of firearms, bows and arrows had become more of a pastime than formerly. These were imported and paid a heavy duty, which makes it probable that it was a sport of the well-to-do. The customs lists of 1612 give the duties as follows: " schooting arrowes the groce . . . 24 li., bowes called hand bowes the dozen, 24 li., bow staves the hundreth, 40 li., bowe stringis the dozen, 5s."

"Rowbowllis" is, of course, the common game of bowls, but as to whether the game was played on a special spot or on any patch of smooth ground there is no early mention. "Penny - stane" is quoits played with a flat stone, a nice useful game which must have needed little preparation, and therefore, it may be surmised, popular with the young.

"Catchepoole" or "kaitchpull" is the French *jeu de paume* or tennis, not the modern lawn-tennis, but the game played in specially prepared courts. There seem to have been a number of these courts in Edinburgh, of which one was reached from Bull's Close, and another situated in the Bishop of Murray's Close, wherever that may have been. An Act of the Dean of Guild's Court in 1547-8 "ordanis Katherein Lyntoun and William Young hir spous to thole and suffer Jonet Turyng, relict of Patrik Flemyng, and hir servandis to have entres in the clos callet the

Byshop of Murrays clos . . . and to gadder up
the kache ballis furth of the said Jonetis kachepell
in tyme to cum quhen it hapins ony to play
thairin." Which makes it seem as though even
then there were bad players whose balls went
where they should not have gone. In the King's
Wark at Leith there was also a tennis court, and
there may have been others in the town not noted.
This was a game at which ladies could play, but
there is no mention of them in connection with
the game in Edinburgh at this early date. Balls
and racquets for the tennis-players were imported,
the former with a duty of 8 li. the hundred, little
enough compared with the duty on golf balls.

But in spite of the desires of the Kirk and the
proclamation of the Council, with its threats of
punishment, the more terrible because they were
indefinite, the Edinburgh men were not easily
dissuaded from their Sunday games. A year
after the proclamation quoted, the Magistrates
found it needful to amplify it in the following
terms :—

"Forswamekle as it is regraitet be the Sessioun
of the Kirk that dyvers inhabitants of this burgh
repaires upoun the Sabboth day to the toun of
Leyth and in tyme of sermonis, and ar sene vagand
athort the streits, drynking in tavernis or otherwayis at golf, archerie or other pastymes upoun
the lynks, thairby profaning the Sabboth day and
gevand evill exampill to others to do the lyke,
thairfor ordanis proclamatioun to be maid . . .

dischairgeing all maner of persouns . . . to be fund upoun the Sabboth day in the toun of Leyth . . . under the payne of warding thair persouns quhill thay pay ane unlaw of fourty schillings and utherwayis be punist in thair persouns."

The girls' games seem to have been very limited, hardly worth the prohibition, for playing ball is the only recreation named for them apart from singing profane songs, which may have been the legendary songs of Scotland, paraphrased out of recognition in the "Gude and Godlie Ballatis." For all that, it may be noted that little girls had their toys. Rattles for children were imported and "babeis or puppettis" which paid 4 li. the gross, so that the imported dolls can have been neither very large nor very costly, unless someone made an undue profit.

The Reformation was responsible for abolishing certain amusements which must have been accessible to all persons in the town, the pageants, religious processions, and public plays. The playfield at the Greenside, originally given for warlike exercises, was used as the ground on which plays were acted, the last of which, apparently, was before the Queen Regent in 1554. There is little said about the pageants and processions, except a mention in the Burgh Court Book of 1508 of the goldsmiths' pageant of the Passion, and a reference in the accounts to a "clerk play" on Corpus Christi. The Records preserve their discreet silence as to the last procession on St Giles' Day, which ended in a notable riot. The old May Day celebrations, with the Abbot of Unreason and Robin Hood, were discountenanced and all attempts to revive them were punished. One luckless Robin Hood was condemned to be hanged, but his fellow - craftsmen rescued him. Thus much amusement passed from the streets of the town. One thing remained: the riding of the marches on All Hallow Even or Trinity Even, as the case might be, must have been a sight for the children of the town, when all burgesses, mounted, assembled at the Provost's lodging with the Magistrates and Council, the Town drummers and trumpeters, and rode in procession round the bounds of the burgh.

Other occasions which must have afforded interest and required preparations by the inhabitants of the burgh were the musters or weapon - showings. Supposed to take place once a year at least, they are recorded only at irregular intervals. After each proclamation of the date of a muster, followed the Act of Council appointing the ensign-bearers. These ensigns should not be confused with the Town's flag, on which a thistle took the place of the figure of St Giles after the Reformation. There were four ensigns, probably one each for the mustering points of the quarters of the Burgh. An Act of Council records the order for new ones: they were made of white taffeta with the Royal arms on one side and the Castle on the other, in black taffeta. Four young

men were appointed to carry them, chosen for each
occasion, and pipers and drummers accompanied the
march. The inhabitants were bound to appear
"bodin in feir of weir" upon the Boroughmuir,
usually at what would be thought now a very early
hour. Towards the end of the sixteenth century
the requisite armour had begun to undergo a
change: the sword remained a part of every
burgess's equipment, almost too much a matter of
course to need mention, the body armour and steel
cap were still usual, mailed gloves were required,
but the halberd and Jeddart axe began to be
supplanted by the hackbut. This is seen in the
Roll of Burgesses, where it figures as the weapon
preferred by would-be burgesses. The custom of
each man providing his own armour seems to
have worked well. Sometimes there was difficulty
owing to the scarcity of armorers, and the
Council found it expedient to grant a pension to
Josias Rikkart, a Flemish armorer, to induce
him to settle in the town to carry on his trade.
But his output did not prove sufficient, for, a few
years later, they found it necessary to send him
to Flanders with a loan to enable him to buy
corslets. On his return they issued a proclamation charging all burgesses to furnish themselves
from Rikkart's new stock at the price of 10 li. So
the weapon-showing must have been a picturesque
and interesting sight, though a matter of grim earnest
to the older participators, who, if they had not

had occasion to use their weapons in actual warfare, must have seen their town overrun with armed men in their youth. It can be imagined a time of great rivalry between quarter and quarter, and trade and craft for the best turned-out men, seeing that it is presumable that the muster ended as a full-dress inspection. The men of Leith took a share in the muster, for two of the incorporations at least, the mariners and the maltmen, marched up and joined the men of Edinburgh. They took the matter with such seriousness that they quarrelled as to precedence in the march, a question settled by the Magistrates, who decreed that the mariners were to march first on the way up and the maltmen first on the way down. History is silent as to the success of the arrangement, so that there is no proof as to whether the judgment contented the *amour propre* of the rivals.

Before passing to a rare but probably a much-admired form of entertainment for the whole inhabitants, it may not be out of place to dwell on the lesser joys of the people. For the most part these would be informal or unauthorised. Some of these would be part of the daily life of the streets: the Town drummer making proclamation of statutes to the sound of his drum up and down the High Street; the sight of a "bairman" or bankrupt sitting on the pillar provided for him at the Market Cross in parti-coloured clothes; the roup of poinded goods carried on by the Town officers at the Cross, where

anything from silk stockings to old Bibles or feather-
beds were offered by order of the Magistrates for
payment of fines or debt.   Then there would be the
sight of the retainers of great houses assembled in
force on a "day of law," otherwise the day on which
their masters' cases were being tried by the Court
of Session, the "bickers" and riots between rival
craftsmen and apprentices, on both of which occasions
part of the show would be the appearance of the
Magistrates and their officers, armed for the fray with
new quarter-staffs, for the suppression of disorder.
Also there were gay young men who found amusement in shooting at the wild birds of the North Loch
from the windows of the houses overlooking it with
hackbuts, and others, still less responsible, who tried
their "dags" or pistols on the High Street and the
wynds and "forestairs" adjoining, an amusement
which once proved fatal to a woman passing by, and
very nearly as disastrous to the unlucky enthusiast over
firearms who caused her death.   Another sight might
be that of a Scots soldier of fortune, in the service
of the Low Countries or of France, allowed to
recruit men for his regiment to the beat of drum :
some adventurous or ne'er-do-weel folk he must
have found, for there never lacked Scots in the wars
on the Continent.   Other street amusements were
furnished with the countenance of the Magistrates.
The forerunner of the barrel-organ may be seen in
the case of a blind man provided by the Council with
a livery of "gros clayth" having the Town's arms on

it, and with a "symphion" to play on. In 1598 the
Council authorised a payment of 10 li. to a tight-
rope walker, "Robert Stewart, master of activity,"
who danced on a rope fastened from the steeple
of St Giles to the head of Joussy's Close. An entry
of the Records in 1607 leaves it doubtful if the
following scheme proposed and turned down was a
novelty or not. If not, it must have been an addition
to the gaiety of the streets. An arrangement was
made with a certain John Orley, Englishman, and
four other expert musicians of his providing, with
musical instruments such as "shalmes" and hautboys
to play through the town between the Castle and the
Netherbow in the morning and at noon, and on the
steeple at six in the evening. For this service he
was to be paid 100 merks yearly, and he and his
men provided with badges bearing the Town arms.
Unfortunately the plan seems to have fallen through,
leaving a suggestion of what would have been
picturesque and attractive if the music had been
good. But to dwell on the possible minor amusements of the town would be to write the complete
history of its doings.

Of other sights which entertained Edinburgh
inhabitants the processions on state occasions cannot
have been the least amusing. Contemporary writers
have described them so thoroughly that there is no
need to dwell on them in detail, but the Treasurer's
Accounts throw light on the official preparations.
It appears from them that most of the performers

must have provided their own costumes, a thing which shows the wealth of the ordinary burgesses. The forty-two, or as others say, twenty-four, young men, "all cled in quhyt talfettie and wisseouris of black collour on thair faces lyk Mores, all full of gold cheynyeis," who danced before Queen Anne at her state entry in 1590, must have provided their own silken clothes and borrowed all the gold chains of their friends to deck themselves for the show. Some of them, according to Calderwood, were attired in cloth of silver, an even more costly material, which was not paid for by the Council. The young women "coastlie apparrelled" who welcomed the Queen at the Butter Tron, must have been dressed by their families; and though the historian does not think fit to be precise as to their dress, other accounts of the period show that the clothes of the well-to-do burgess women could be very fine. The Council furnished some costumes, which were more fantastic. The accounts tell of the painting of the globe from which a small boy presented the keys of the good town to the Queen, and of the fourteen crowns and sceptres made by the official painter, John Workman. He also provided painted coats-of-arms. There were Highland and sword dances, though no sufficient description allows of stating exactly what they were. All that is known is that a certain David Paterson received 50s. for making seventeen sets of Highland men's clothes. The sword dance sounds as though it may have been akin to Morris dancing, for the preparations included the purchase of twelve pairs of white shoes, twelve hats of flowers, bells and painted belts. A bill was presented for buckram for "making the nympheis clais" and another for "painting of Bachus," who sat at the Market Cross at a fountain running wine and drank the King's health, a post for which there was surely much competition, and the painting of Hercules' baton and rod. The putting up of streamers on the steeple on the day of the Queen's entry cost 20s., and the hanging of tapestry in St Giles, painting the Royal gallery, strewing flowers and grass in the church, and burning "rossett" there to drown less pleasant odours came to the modest sum of 7 li. 17s. It was a pleasing time for the workmen, for the Council encouraged diligence in a way they could understand.

"Item, for drink to our haill warkmen this oulk bygane at morn and eftirnone to hald thame to thair wark for expeditioun of the samyn, ilk day thre gallounis aill at Vs. VIId. the galloun . . 4 li. 16s."

Being pressed for time, the wrights and other workmen continued their operations in the church for thirty-six hours on end, and lighting was provided by two poor boys who held candles for them, being paid two shillings for their night's work. On this occasion four quarts of ale and two loaves were given for their refreshment. The next day the men who hung the tapestry finished off two quarts of wine and two loaves of "manchet" bread, provided in

THE BOROUGH MUIR AND MERCHISTON CASTLE

160

case the "strangers" should be hungry in church during the sermon.

This festival finished in satisfactory fashion for the young and undignified with the scattering of twelve boxes of "scrochertis and confectis" from the stairs of the Bow. This was surely the best part of the whole day for the children in a time when sweet foods were a luxury and not a commonplace of life.

This, it is true, was only one of many such shows, but they did resemble each other broadly, and being for the most part well described elsewhere, it does not seem worth while to record more than one example.

A form of entertainment to which the Council were addicted was the banquet. They never seem to have raised any objection to playing the host to the King or to his foreign guests, ambassadors or visiting celebrities, and yet the feasts provided can have been no little care. It is true that the Common Good or a tax on all burgesses met the expenses, so that the Council were not out of pocket and even had their losses in household goods replaced.

Whether it is fair to take any particular period as typical of the rest is uncertain, so that it need not be imagined that the Council's entertainments between 1589 and 1603 are an example of the amount of hospitality extended to the King and to strangers. These years included the King's marriage and a serious dispute between James VI. and the Magistrates over Kirk affairs. Both required banquets, one of welcome to the new Queen, the other of reconciliation with his Majesty, who had had it all his own way. There was a dinner to the Danish envoys who came with the Queen; "a collatioun" and a supper to the King, when peaceful relations between him and the Council had been restored; a banquet to the Queen's brother, the Duke of Holstein, and another to the French ambassador, De Rohan. The Treasurer's Accounts are a mine of information for such affairs : they only stop short of the actual menu, but all the ingredients of the meals are recorded in the greatest detail.

On the occasion of the arrival of the Queen, the Council were anxious to make as good an impression as possible on the Danes : drastic measures were taken to ensure clean streets, no beggars were allowed to be near, men worked overtime on the cleaning of St Giles. The Magistrates made a house-to-house levy among themselves of the best of their own plenishings to furnish forth the inevitable banquet, including napery, cupboards of plate, dishes and other ornaments.

Perhaps it is worth while to remember that our forefathers were hearty eaters. True they restricted themselves to three meals a day, but Parliament had thought necessary to restrain them further. The ninth Parliament of James VI. forbade the eating of meat on Wednesday, Friday and Saturday, as well as in Lent, a period fixed by law since it was no longer set by the Church. An earlier Parliament, Queen Mary, 1551, laid down the number of dishes

Rationing and Feasting

of meat which a man might have for dinner, stating that legislation was necessary because of dearth. The allowance is worth noting by a generation which knows what rationing is. An archbishop, bishop, or earl might have eight dishes of meat; abbots, lords, priors and deans, six dishes; barons and freeholders, four dishes; burgesses and "uther substantious men spiritual and temporal," three dishes, and in every case only one kind of meat in each dish. If this was dearth, what was plenty!

The reconciliation of the King with the Town, after their quarrel in 1596-97, was sealed by two meals, among other things. The "desert" on his entry into the town in friendship was not expensive overmuch, a mere trifle costing 62 li. 1s. But the supper, which took place a few days later, was more ambitious. The account for the meal runs as follows :—

"To Thomas Brounrig for furneising of all storis of flesche and wyld meit . . . 64 li. 18s.
For colis (coals) to the supper . 4 li.
For ane barrell aill with sum breid . 2 li. 17s. 6d.
For walx candill . . . 36s.
For uther candill . . . 10s.
Payit to the suckerman for his desert 23 li. 6s.
To Mungo Ros for his potafrie . 13 li. 10s.
For wyne and beir with veschell . 50 li.
For VI quartis of gallok wyne . 6 li.
For nakketis and mayne breid . 4 li. 15s.
For II plaitis that was tint . . 3 li. 6s. 8d."

The Amusements of Edinburgh

Which came to a total of 181 li. 16s. 4d. Even those who did not love James VI. admitted that he was temperate in eating and drinking, therefore the provision must have included his attendants, unless the Council finished off the repast after his Majesty was satisfied.

In 1598 the Duke of Holstein came to Scotland to visit the King and Queen. The Council was invited to entertain him, and proceeded to spend 1103 li. 18s. 4d. upon the feast. The house occupied by Ninian Macmorane, built by his brother John in 1590, was chosen for the banquet, and the Accounts record the preparations. Most of the money went on food, though a few entries concern the replacing of linen napkins, borrowed for the occasion, and lost; the payment of 13 li. 6s. 8d. to trumpeters, and of 9 li. to minstrels, and to two Frenchmen, "quha handelit and dressit" the napery, to two school-masters of 5 li., presumably for orations of some sort, to the Queen's master cook of 10 li., and for transporting dishes and water to the house for the cooks.

As on most similar occasions, the drink was abundant. It included two puncheons of wine at a cost of 136 li., five gallons and a quart of claret, 21 li., seven quarts of wine, 7 li., with payment to two apothecaries for making it into hypocras, 11 li. 15s., a tun of English beer, 13 li. 4s. 8d., four barrels of ale, 3 li. 6s. 8d.

The food included "foullis wyld and tame," at a

cost of 212 li. 18s. 8d.; venison, two hams, turkeys, which from the difficulty met with in obtaining them must have been rare, and meat at 60 li. 6s. 8d. The baker's account came to 129 li. 6s.; the confectioner's, 184 li.; thirty oranges cost 30s. and twenty-five apples, 6s. 8d. Four stone of fresh and one of salt butter cost 14 li. 13s. 4d.; verjuice and rose-water, 11s.; flowers and herbs, 7 li. 3s. 4d. Other materials provided for the cooks include olive oil, or, as they wrote it, "uldolie," raisins, peas, saffron, cinnamon, and five dozen eggs and a quire of paper, presumably for decoration.

There were many other banquets, but none are given in more detail than this one, which is the excuse for dealing with it at so great length.

With such doings it is possible to assume that life in the capital of Scotland could never have been exactly dull, and might compare favourably with the present day, when, though better conditions prevail, life at times has less of the shows which amused the inhabitants of more than three hundred years ago.

CHAPTER VII

THE SETT OF THE BURGH

ONE of our early historians asserts that the Castle of Edinburgh was built by Camelon, King of the Picts, and that in the fierce and frequent wars with the Picts, Danes, Romans and English, the city was often destroyed and her monuments and early charters irretrievably lost. The blanks in our early history have been supplied by the inventions of numerous writers; and there have been occasions when the sanction of authority has been given to statements on this speculative subject. For example, when King James VI. returned to his native land in 1618, it is recorded that the Magistrates of Edinburgh welcomed him in a congratulatory Harangue, in the course of which they asserted, with much courage, that their city had been founded three hundred and thirty years before the incarnation of Christ. After the same manner it is solemnly maintained in an Act of Parliament, of date 23rd April 1685, that the Scottish nation had, for a period of 2000 years, been ruled by the sceptre of 111 monarchs.

It may be admitted that these official statements

are untrustworthy and that the origin of the city cannot be discovered. Its existence, however, may be inferred in the time of King David I., who reigned from 1124 to 1153, and who is said to have held his Court in the Castle. In one of the Charters which this King granted to the Abbey of Holyrood about the middle of the twelfth century, it is stated that the King conveys a certain portion of the revenue which he draws from his "Burgh of Edwinsburg," and also a large toft or holding of land in the burgh, which is to be held with the same privileges as those enjoyed by his own burgesses. In virtue of this charter the Abbot was empowered to establish between the Abbey of Holyrood and the Burgh of Edinburgh a new burghal territory which afterwards became the Canongate burgh of regality.

At this period of time it is assumed that the community as such was not recognised as forming a corporate body. A populous place is not of necessity a burgh in the legal sense, and, according to our modern Statutes, such a place must follow certain procedure and become incorporated before it attains the status of a burgh. At the period of King David's charter, the burgesses of Edinburgh had not been erected into a legal corporation, yet it is not doubted that they possessed, even then, certain privileges in respect of trade and commerce, and that in return for his holding of property each burgess paid a rent or maill to the Crown, which in the reign of King David is stated to have been at the rate of 5d. for each rood of land. These rents, or *firmæ burgales*, were collected by bailies, not bailies in the modern sense of the word, but rather bailiffs or stewards, or as we might call them, tax-gatherers, appointed by the Crown. These royal officers appear to have possessed certain administrative and judicial powers, and they accounted in exchequer not only for the rents which they ingathered but also for the *exitus curiæ* or fines collected in the Courts of Justice, and for the customs and dues levied on merchandise. In the accounting, allowances fell to be made in respect of rents not ingathered, or written off as bad debts, and for payments made in obedience to Royal Command or otherwise, as in the case of Holyrood which has been mentioned.

This continued to be the ordinary practice down to the closing years of the reign of King Robert the Bruce, when the system, already in existence in England, began to be copied in Scotland. The system opened up a new chapter in burghal history, in which the community as such was recognised for the first time; and, to the communities so recognised, grants were made of the burghs themselves with all their privileges and immunities, to be holden of the Crown for payment of fixed feu-duties in commutation of those fluctuating payments, which resulted upon a balancing of accounts between the bailies and the Great Chamberlain. It is one of the indications of the early importance of Edinburgh that it appears to have been among the first of the burghs to obtain a charter of this description. This well-known charter is dated in 1329, and is the earliest city charter now extant. It recognises the community of the burgh as a corporate body holding territory and privileges by direct grant from the Crown, and confirms to them all rights as held by them in the reign of King Alexander III. It also provides for a rent or annual payment of 52 merks sterling (£34, 13s. 4d.), as payable from the corporation to the King. Thereafter the rents or maills, due by the burgesses for their several tofts or tenements, became payable to the corporation as assignees of the Crown, and the corporation in turn paid over the 52 merks referred to, under deduction of certain allowances adjusted from time to time. Down to the present day the corporation continues to pay to the Crown the sum of £5 sterling under this charter as the portion of the annual payment which still remains as not having been allowed in deduction by the Exchequer. When Royal Burghs were fully developed, the titles of individual burgesses were made out by the town's officials, and the properties were described as being held of the Sovereign in free burgage for services of burgh used and wont. In process of time the payments of feu-duty by the individual burgesses ceased and burgage property became free of feu-duties or casualties.

The Sett of the Burgh

On this subject historians have differed and no clear light can be derived from the older muniments

Early Forms of Local Government.

of the country. In the case of Royal Burghs it has been inferred that the powers of local government were at first committed to those persons nominated by the Crown who were the original bailies of the burghs. These officials acted as stewards or collectors of the revenues payable to the Crown, and appear also to have exercised the petty jurisdiction necessary for maintaining peace and good order.

At what period the inhabitants of Royal Burghs were emancipated so far as to have any share in the choice of their own rulers is a subject for conjecture. The earliest collection or code of burghal laws is known as the *Leges Burgorum,* and is said to have been sanctioned by the legislature in the reign of King David I. This code provides that there should be three head courts yearly within burgh "at the whilk all burgesses sould compeir"; and again, that at the first head court after Michaelmas, "the bailies sould be chosen of faithfull men and of gude fame be the common consent of the honest men of the burgh." It is doubtful whether this procedure was law in the reign of King David when the burgesses paid their rents or maills to the King's bailie, and the burghs had not been erected into corporate bodies; but it formed a part of the constitution of Burghs Royal in the fourteenth century, as is established by manuscripts of that period. The probability seems to be that this stage of independence was reached when the burghs came to be incorporated and recognised as forming one of the estates of the realm, with the obligation to make contributions to general aids and impositions.

The *Leges Burgorum* make no reference to the body of men now known as councillors. Another compilation known as the *Statuta Gildæ*, to which the date 1284 has been assigned, contains a regulation in regard to these appointments : "We statute that the common counsell and communitie sall be governed by 24 gude men, best, maist discreit and maist faithfull within the burgh, chosen to that effect together with the mayor and four baillies"; and again, "be the sicht and consideration of the communitie." These and similar enactments are taken as implying that the whole corporate rights of the burgh, including the right of electing the Magistrates and Councillors, were vested in the burgesses at large; and that at this early period the elections were made at head courts by general poll.

The earliest records of Edinburgh do not, however, disclose the existence here of this simple, democratic system, though they make numerous references to head courts. It would appear that by the beginning of the fifteenth century municipal power was a monopoly of the merchants and traders of this burgh. One of the purposes for which burghs were fostered was to promote the trade of the country; and the mercantile classes naturally benefited most from the monopoly of commerce which was a peculiar feature of mediæval life. From early times there seems to have existed a Merchant Guild, and this organised body not only attended to matters of trade, but assumed the right to manage the whole affairs of the community. The *Statuta Gildæ* have been mentioned above, and this code provided for the election of officers of the guild, including a council of twelve called the dusane or *duodecim consules.* In course of time the number of members forming this council largely exceeded the original limit of twelve.

If one refers to the printed extracts from the Records of the city it will be found that the first item is dated 3rd October 1403, and relates to the election of officers of the guild. "The first head court held after the feast of Saint Michael in the Tolbuith of the burgh of Edinburgh the brethren of the guild being called and compearing; the officers of the guild were elected as follows:—*Prepositus,* Alexander Naper; *Decanus gilde et custoditor operis ecclesie,* Symon de Schele; *Ballivus de Leyth,* Joannes Robertsoun; *Thesaurius,* Joannes Lamb"; then follow two officers of the guild; tasters of flesh and wine; and a Council of 45 members whose names are given. It has been commented that in this Minute the guildry are regarded as identical with the burgesses and are the only electors; and that the officers chosen by them are the Magistrates and Town Council who are to govern the community and manage its affairs for the year. Apparently, at this date, the local government of the burgh was entirely in the hands of the merchant burgesses and the guildry affairs were treated as identical with those of the community.

While the merchants were thus monopolising the conduct of public affairs, the artisans or craftsmen were growing in numbers and wealth, and the time came when the latter did not willingly submit to be excluded altogether from municipal privileges. The merchants were the higher rank, being burgesses and guild brethren, while the craftsmen held what was called the single burgess ticket. Before the end of the thirteenth century, the craftsmen had begun to form themselves into associations, and during the next two centuries their combinations became more definite. It was part of the policy of mediæval times to foster handicrafts and to give exclusive privileges to organised bodies of skilled artisans. In Edinburgh, the various crafts were incorporated by the Town Council under Seals of Cause; and in this way fourteen trade or craft incorporations were formed between 1449 and 1581. The result of this policy was to give rise to a prolonged conflict between the merchants and the craftsmen; the latter being determined to secure a share in the management of municipal affairs, which was then the exclusive enjoyment of the merchant classes, notwithstanding the old laws to which reference has been made.

In this state of matters it is recorded that the elections led to "gret truble and contensione yeirly throw the multitud and clamor of the commins simpil personis." The election evils complained of led to the passing of an Act in 1469 in the reign of King James III., which forms a landmark in the burghal history of Scotland, subverting, as it did, the original basis of popular election, and forming, as we should now suppose, a surprising remedy to offer to the people of the country.

Before dealing with this Act it may be proper to comment that the oldest officer in the burgh The Officers of was apparently the one known by the the Burgh. familiar name of Bailie. In the first stage he was the bailiff, the agent or representative nominated by the Crown. When the burgh became incorporated it was no longer necessary for the King to appoint a deputy, but the old name was continued and transferred to the representative of the community by whom he was chosen. The *Statuta Gildæ* contemplated the election of four bailies annually to represent the four wards or quarters of the burgh. This number is not usually given in the earliest Minutes of the Town Council, but it became the invariable rule in the course of the sixteenth century, and Edinburgh possessed four bailies and no more right down to the year 1856.

In the Burgh Laws mention is made of the

mayor, alderman, or *prepositus*, the last of these terms being used at times in reference to a single person, but also at times in the plural, referring apparently to the bailies. It does not appear that the chief magistrate of Edinburgh was ever called " Mayor "; but in the older records he was styled " Alderman," and apparently the first use of " *Prepositus* " in the sense of Provost occurred in 1377, these terms being regarded as synonymous. In some years the chief magistrate was designated " President." The title of "Alderman" occurs intermittently down to 1439; that of " *Prepositus* " down to 1530; that of " President " down to 1558; thereafter there has been a constant usage of the modern title of " Provost." The first known application of the title of " Lord Provost " occurred in 1487 when the office was held by a nobleman, Patrick Hepburn, Lord Hales. In December 1514 the expression "principal provost" occurs in the Council Minutes, and in 1518 there is a reference to the "provost, president and bailies."

The Dean of Guild is another officer of high antiquity, and at one time the office was regarded as the stepping-stone to the Provostship. Nothing is known of the original constitution or charter of the Guildry in Edinburgh, which may have been based upon the *Statuta Gildæ* of 1284, but there is no doubt that at one stage this body held the leading position of power in the burgh. According to one school of writers the Guilds provided the first form of municipal authority in Scotland, and certainly the early information concerning burghs is intimately connected with the Guilds. In this view the Guildry is perhaps the very oldest institution in the city.

It is clear from the quotation given above that in the year 1403 the Provost and other Magistrates of Edinburgh were appointed by the brethren of the Guildry. At this early period the Dean of Guild probably had the regulation of questions concerning the affairs of the merchant burgesses, trade and shipping, and the erection of buildings. In the course of the fifteenth century there was a transformation in the public life of the burgh, as the result of which the Guildry lost their power and standing as a corporate body. In 1496 the Town Council appropriated their funds and certain of their privileges, and also assumed the right to control the appointment of the Dean of Guild. Thereafter for some three and a half centuries the influence and power of the Guildry were in abeyance, and the right to appoint its own head was only restored to it by the Municipal Reform Act of 1833.

The Provost, four Bailies, and Dean of Guild were Magistrates, as was also the Treasurer, whose office from its nature originated probably with the first erection of the burgh as a corporate body. The first known reference to the Treasurer occurs in 1403 in the Minute already quoted.

Frequent reference to the "dusane" occur in the early Minutes, and these appear to identify

The Old Tolbooth

the "dusane" with the Councillors. In June 1490 there is a reference to deacons as acting along with the Council. Subsequent to 1500 the Acts of Council usually bear to have been passed by the Provost, Bailies, and Council.

A question sometimes arises as to the order in which members of Council should be placed in processions or on ceremonial occasions. This order of precedence had been regulated by long practice, but was expressed definitely by a Minute of Council of 14th October 1625. In the early Charters the gift is sometimes expressed in favour of the burgesses and community, sometimes it is made to the Provost, Bailies, and community. The first Charter to give names and details is the well-known Charter of 1482, which sets out the order following, viz. :—Provost, Bailies, Dean of Guild, Treasurer, Common Clerk, twelve Councillors. This continues to be the order of precedence excepting for the City Chamberlain and the Convener of Trades, who are of later date as will be mentioned below.

Commenting on the Act of 1469 and its application to Edinburgh, Sir Thomas Hunter states that it provided (1) that office-bearers and members of Council should only hold office for a year; (2) that the retiring Council should choose their successors, the new Council; (3) that the retiring Council and the new Council together should choose the office-bearers for the coming year—namely, Alderman, Dean of Guild, etc.; and (4) that, in the election of office-bearers, one person from each of the trade incorporations should vote along with the old and new Council. The ancient rights of the citizens or burgesses were thus arbitrarily taken away, and what has been called "an entail of municipal rule and influence" was practically established. The old Council would naturally choose their own friends or dependants, who, in due time, returned the compliment, although to some extent the craftsmen were recognised. The position was not made any better by the Act of 1474, which provided that four of the members of the old Council should always be re-elected to the new. These Acts inaugurated a system of close and secret administration of burgh affairs which led to almost continual conflict. Instead of the old custom of the Provost, Magistrates, and Councillors being elected at the head guild annually by the merchant burgesses, the election became very much one of rotation of a limited number of individuals, so that the Town Council was practically a close corporation, self-elected.

In the year 1552 there were two craftsmen in the Council, which then consisted of twelve members, probably the Provost, four Bailies, Dean of Guild, Treasurer, three merchants, and two craftsmen. In 1559 the Queen Regent, Mary of Lorraine, sent an order to the Town Council requiring them to admit the votes of eleven deacons in the various steps of the elections of that year; but the Council "could yield no obedience to the order for it was contrary to the Act of Parliament." In 1582 the craftsmen or trades had obtained such a footing in the Council that the mutual squabbles between them and the merchants filled the city with tumults, till at length both parties, with a view to obtaining a decisive settlement, referred their various claims to King James VI. by whose decision or decreet arbitral the sett or municipal constitution of the town was established upon a basis which it substantially retained down to the year 1833. By this well-known decreet the Town Council was appointed to consist of twenty-five members, viz.:—(1) seven Magistrates of the estate and calling of merchants, namely the Provost, four Bailies, Dean of Guild, and Treasurer; (2) ten merchants, namely, the Old Provost, four Old Bailies, Dean of Guild and Treasurer of the year preceding, and three others; (3) eight craftsmen, namely, six deacons and two others. The fourteen incorporations were each to have a deacon, to be chosen out of a leet of three members nominated by the Town Council, a system which restricted the freedom of the craftsmen. Six of these deacons were to become ordinary members of the Town Council, and the other eight were extraordinary deacons, who were given a right to vote with the Town Council on certain subjects. Leets were also to be made of

candidates for the various offices in the Town
Council, and in making these appointments and
filling up vacancies the old and new Council voted
together. An equal number of merchants and
craftsmen were to be chosen as Auditors of the
Town's Accounts ; and craftsmen as well as merchants
were to be admitted guild brethren.

It may be mentioned that the Magistrates and
Merchant Councillors were generally chosen from
the members of the Merchant Company after the
incorporation of this body in 1681.

The sett as fixed in 1583 was modified on at
least three occasions. Notwithstanding its terms
and the terms of the Act of 1469 which prohibited
all magistrates from continuing in office longer than
two years together, a different practice prevailed
which amounted to an abuse of power. In 1658
the Town Council passed an Act to provide that
Magistrates should not be elected or continued longer
than one or at most two years together at one time.
In 1673 this Act was revived and approved, and it
was ordained that the Magistrates should "take an
oath for the inviolably observing of the said Act in
all time coming."

The trades were never satisfied with the sett
and made continual efforts to extend their power,
one of their demands being that their Convener
should be received into the Town Council in that
character ; another being that the extraordinary
deacons should be allowed to vote on a large number

of subjects. In the early years of the eighteenth century their accumulated demands alarmed the merchants and resulted in the two factions bringing cross actions in the Court of Session. The dispute was carried on for nearly ten years, till both parties thought proper to submit their differences to the decision of Archibald, Earl of Islay, afterwards Duke of Argyle, who in 1730 pronounced a decreet arbitral by which, according to Maitland, peace and concord were happily restored. By this decreet the office of Deacon Convener, which had been instituted in 1578, was officially recognised, and this officer obtained a seat in the Town Council which, as we know, he still enjoys. A new method of leeting for the deacons was also recognised; and the extraordinary deacons, eight in number, were given extended rights of voting in the Town Council.

The sett or constitution of the burgh was therefore contained in the decreets arbitral given in 1583 and 1730 in conjunction with the Acts of Council of 1658 and 1673.

The annual election took place at Michaelmas and was spread over three weeks. It began by a warning, as it was called, given to **The Old Elections.** each of the fourteen incorporations to make up leets of six of their members with a view to the selection of deacons. On the same day, according to ancient usage the Council received for their year's attendance the following sums, viz. :—the Lord Provost, £1, 11s. 6d. ; the four

Bailies, 10s. 6d. each, and 10s. in addition for Sheriff's gloves; the Dean of Guild and Treasurer each 10s. 6d.; and the remaining ten merchants, eight ordinary and eight extraordinary Trades members, 3s. 6d. each.

The leets for deacons then came before the Town Council, who reduced them from six to three, out of which each incorporation chose its new deacon. At this stage the incorporations dined together, the old and new deacons being present; and this occasion was known as the " showing of faces."

Out of the fourteen deacons thus chosen the Town Council chose six as Council deacons, these generally being taken from the extraordinary deacons of the year preceding. Thereupon a meeting was held in the Magdalen Chapel, when one of the six was elected as Deacon Convener. Another entertainment followed, termed the Convener's dinner, at which the Blue Blanket was conspicuously displayed and afterwards committed to the charge of the new Convener.

A day or two later the Council met again for the election of the three Merchant Councillors and the two Trades Councillors, the Town Council being thus augmented from 25 to 30 for the time being. At the next meeting leets were made up, out of which the Lord Provost, Magistrates, Dean of Guild, and Treasurer were chosen, the old and new Council of 30 and the 8 extraordinary deacons all voting together. The office-bearers of the preceding year

The Manner of the Elections

became Old Provost, Old Bailies, Old Dean of Guild and Old Treasurer, but if any had retired other members were appointed to the vacant offices. This business being finished, the three Old Merchants and two Old Trades Councillors retired, and the Council of 25 was thus completed.

The election was followed by a splendid entertainment to which illustrious strangers were freely invited and the expense was defrayed from the City funds. Thus we read that in 1820 the election dinner of the Magistrates cost £533 sterling.

On the day when the Council was filled up, the Admiral of Leith, and the baron bailies of Canongate, Calton, and Portsburgh were appointed, these officers being generally chosen from the Old Bailies. The resident bailies in the places named were also appointed, these being chosen from among the most respectable inhabitants. On the same day also the Captain of the Orange Colours was appointed, the first Merchant Councillor being generally complimented with this title.

After 1730 the extraordinary deacons, eight in number, had right to vote, not only in elections, but in the grants of feus and tacks, and the expenditure of the common good. Before the end of the eighteenth century the matters requiring their attention were of frequent occurrence and they were summoned to attend all meetings and only disqualified from voting in a few cases. Consequently meetings of the ordinary Council became the exception and not the rule ; and the membership while nominally 25 was generally 33 in practice.

Maitland mentions that in the eighteenth century the Council met weekly on Wednesday when the business of the day was introduced by a suitable prayer, which had been composed by a bailie so far back as 1590, and which he quotes at length. He adds that if this prayer is laid aside the Council accept of such an one as one of the city ministers is pleased to give them.

The close corporation, in spite of the threats and maledictions of critics and reformers, had a career of more than three-and-a-half centuries, and inevitably in this long stretch of time many things happened which might be mentioned in a narrative more detailed than the present one. So long as the King resided at Holyrood the Town Council in their elections and administration were exposed to *force majeure* from the Court ; for example, King James provided a list of the individuals to be chosen at the elections of 1584, and stated in his letter " herein we lippin to be satisfied our request being so reasonable." The Stuart Kings were prone to exercise arbitrary power in local affairs even from London. In 1634 the Provost and other office-bearers were elected in compliance with a mandate from King Charles I. His successor, King Charles II., interdicted the annual elections in 1674, and shortly thereafter certain bailies were forced on the Council by

The City Chamberlain and Other Subjects.

command of the King; and other instances of royal intervention might be cited. When King William ascended the throne, the Royal Burghs, including Edinburgh, were required to choose a new set of Magistrates by a poll of all the burgesses. Again, after the event of 1745 the King issued a Royal Warrant authorising the burgesses to make a new election by a poll.

The first reference to a Chamberlain appears in 1700, when Mr Thomas Fisher was appointed with this title to act as assistant to the Treasurer in the collection and management of the city revenues. The office was, however, deemed to be superfluous and was discontinued about nine years thereafter.

In the middle of the century the New Town began to arise, and, with the increases in revenue and expenditure, it became necessary to give some assistance to the Treasurer. That official only held office for two consecutive years and could not be expected to possess a complete knowledge of the town's affairs. In 1766 the proposal was made to employ a Chamberlain or factor, and a Committee having considered the proposal, reported that it would be "attended with the happiest consequences to have the city's revenues managed by a man of integrity and application in the character of a Chamberlain." The Council approved of this recommendation, and thereupon appointed Hugh Buchan, writer, to be Chamberlain to the good town, during their pleasure. Mr Buchan held his office until 1796, when he retired on a pension. His successor was Thomas Hay, about whose appointment there was some difficulty, and a motion was carried in Council to the effect that the Chamberlain of the City should be annually elected, and that the office should be declared vacant each year. In 1804 Mr Hay resigned his office, and the then Treasurer, John Jackson, was appointed during pleasure with a salary of £600.

Mr Jackson having resigned in 1809, the next Chamberlain was Thomas Henderson, then holding the office of Old Treasurer in the Council. His appointment was declared to be *ad vitam aut culpam*, and this departure from precedent led to a long dispute and to a litigation in the Court of Session, as the result of which his election was reduced. Mr Henderson having acquiesced in the decision, the Town Council re-elected him to the office during their pleasure.

The next Chamberlain was John Turnbull, Dean of Guild, appointed in 1822, this being the third instance of the office going to a member of the Town Council. Thereafter the following appointments have been made: in 1838, Mr David Irons Robertson; in 1872, Mr Robert Adam; in 1895, Mr Robert Paton; in 1925, Mr John D. Imrie.

Turning now to another topic, it may be of interest to mention that from early times it had been the custom to allow the Provost to receive certain fees and perquisites. The first occasion on which a direct vote of money was made to him appears to

have been in 1478, when the Committee allowed him
£20 out of the common purse to his fee "for honour
and worship of the toune." In 1520 the Provost
received a grant of 100 merks of the common good,
besides the ordinary fee, for the sustentation of four
servants to bear halberts with him for a year, because
"the world is brukle and troublous." It has been
asserted that this was the first occasion when
halberts were carried in civic processions.

In 1718 the Council passed an Act settling an
annual salary of £300 on the Lord Provost for
" maintaining the dignity of the chair." The Act
narrates the inconveniences that had arisen on
account of certain practices attending payments
then being made to the Lord Provost "from the
secret acknowledgments made in money or otherwise
by persons who come into lucrative offices; and
from the gratuities of the same kind given by those
who obtain feus or tacks of houses, lands and other
branches of the town's revenues." The salary was
given in lieu thereof, and it was provided that at
the end of each year the Lord Provost should give a
long oath in a prescribed form to the effect that
he had not received any other monies directly or
indirectly. The salary was increased to £500 in 1771
" by reason of the great rise in the price of provisions,
especially of wines, and also of house rents, and the
different manner of entertaining since the salary of
£300 was fixed." The salary was increased to £800
in 1805 and to £1000 in 1817.

The Sett of the Burgh

The income of the burgh came from the Common Good and generally from that source alone, so that the lives of the burgesses were not made unhappy by the imposition of rates grievous to be borne, with the prospect that they were to become more grievous still. This income consisted of feu-duties, casualties and rents, customs of trades and markets, harbour dues and fines of Court. Upon inland traffic of all sorts, however trifling in its amount, there existed from a very early period a system of petty exactions, and in every market and fair within the liberties of the burgh extreme vigilance was maintained to prevent the untaxed transfer of the most common commodities. From this source came the petty customs and market dues, some of which survive to the present day. In addition the Royal Burghs enjoyed a complete monopoly of foreign trade, a mediæval conception which was the cause of the trouble with Leith. The high value attached to these trading privileges may in some degree be estimated by the extreme jealousy and care with which, from the earliest times, they were maintained and vindicated against all encroachments and by the numberless confirmations and regulations of which they were the subject.

The Town Council of former days was not embarrassed by any self-denying ordinance; on the contrary, when any public work was to be undertaken a preference was given to councillors as a matter of course; and the same favour was extended in respect of public appointments. The deacons of trades were

Collectors for the King

ex officio members of Council and these offices were matters of keen contest, being in fact worth a good deal of money. The deacon of the masons claimed as a right to be employed as builder to the Corporation and to charge his own prices without check. The other deacons expected like favours and thus things went comfortably round until interrupted by the advent of burgh reform.

The Royal Burghs were required to collect and pay over to the Crown a certain yearly sum in name of cess or land tax. The proportion falling to Edinburgh was latterly £2600 or thereby; and in the collection of this impost the bailies maintained the old tradition of being collectors for the King. In addition there were local taxes known as "stents" and ingathered by officials known as "stent masters." A perusal of the printed Records of Edinburgh will show that in early times the bailies assumed the right to stent the burgesses for any purpose and to an indefinite amount. This arbitrary power was restrained in the middle of the seventeenth century by certain decisions of the Courts which laid down the conditions under which stents should be imposed. One of these required that the stents should be imposed at a head court or assembly of the whole burgesses and inhabitants convened by ringing of a bell or tuck of a drum. In these head courts, lawfully fenced, the bailies presided and the resolution to proceed with the stents required to be approved by the majority of those present.

The Sett of the Burgh

The stents thus became voluntary, and inevitably difficulties arose in enforcing payment from unwilling citizens, the result of which was that this old power ceased to be exercised and fell gradually into disuse. In Edinburgh certain stents continued to be levied in virtue of Acts of Parliament, but the principle of no taxation without representation was apprehended in a local as well as in a national sense. The Town Council was an unrepresentative body and the people would not therefore have tolerated an imposition by them apart from statutory powers. Obviously, however, local government in a modern sense could not have been built up on a basis so narrow and insufficient as the Common Good alone. Its foundation in a financial sense is the levy of rates and assessments, that is the moneys raised from the citizens for specific purposes and applied exclusively to these purposes. It is here that the line falls to be drawn between the old and the new in local government.

Towards the end of the eighteenth century the people of Scotland began to be conscious of the fact **The Police Commissioners.** that the system under which they lived had gone on unchanged since mediæval days. Now, however, a desire was taking shape for something better in the way of public services, and aspirations filled the minds of the people to have public water supplies instead of private wells; to have the roadways broader and safer; to light and pave the streets; to enjoy the benefit of an effective system of police; and, as a necessary condition to have popularly elected Commissioners, with powers to raise money by way of assessments. Hence from the end of the eighteenth century onwards, numerous private Acts of Parliament were obtained by the larger communities of Scotland for these and the like purposes, and the execution of such Acts was committed, not to Town Councils, but either to special trusts or to bodies of men more or less representative of the people, who afterwards came to be known generally as Police Commissioners. Lord Cockburn states that this establishment was the first example of popular election in Scotland, and was welcomed as a "divine institution" when first introduced.

The first local Statute of the description referred to did not relate to the royalty, but to certain districts on the south side, eight in number, called the Southern districts. These districts were named as follows :—(1) Teviot Row and Lauriston; (2) Bristo and Potterrow; (3) George Square; (4) Nicolson's Park; (5) Crosscauseway; (6) Gibbet Street; (7) Causewayside; (8) Tollcross. Each district was put under the charge of five Commissioners, certain of them being nominated, and each had a Treasurer, Collector, and Clerk. The Act made provision for cleansing, lighting, and watching the streets and ways, and for removing nuisances and annoyances, and it gave power to assess the occupiers of houses and shops in a sum not exceeding 6d. per £ of real rent.

The Sett of the Burgh

This Statute was obtained in 1771, and in the following year another followed, giving powers for lighting, cleansing, and watching the districts of Canongate, Pleasance, and Leith Wynd, and for imposing a rate not exceeding 2½ per cent. of the real rents of premises.

In 1785 an Act was passed for extending the royalty of the city and dividing it into two districts, called the ancient and extended royalty, and for various other purposes. The Commissioners therein appointed were empowered to assess to the extent of 2 per cent. on the valued rents of premises for lighting purposes. Each district had fifteen Commissioners with a Collector and Clerk. The line of division between the ancient and extended royalties was defined as the keystone of the middle arch of the North Bridge running east to the Trinity College Church and west to the north side of the Castle, along the middle of the low ground formerly the North Loch.

In 1805 an Act was passed for regulating the Police of the city and adjoining districts, and for other purposes. This superseded the earlier Acts in respect of watching, reduced the old Town Guard from 126 to 37 men, and introduced a general and uniform system of Police. The establishment had an office in Riddle's Court, Lawnmarket, and was placed under the management of Commissioners, partly official and partly elected by householders having a certain qualification. The area under their charge was divided into six districts or wards, and included the burgh as extended, and also Canongate, Pleasance, Calton, precincts of the Abbey, Abbey-hill, Picardy, the eastern and western roads to Leith, the eight southern districts, and all other places within the toll-bars erected on the high roads leading to the city, and the villages of Canonmills, Water of Leith, Restalrig, Jock's Lodge, and Portobello. The assessment was limited to 3 per cent., a superintendent was appointed with wide powers who also officiated in the Police Court, and the Act was to continue in force for ten years.

In 1812 another Act was passed for regulating the Police of the city and adjoining districts. The preamble stated that the regulations established by the previous Acts had been found upon trial to be ineffectual for the preservation of peace and good order, and that it was expedient that one uniform system of Police should be established, whereby a single body of Commissioners might be entrusted, not only with the duty of watching and protecting the inhabitants within the limits prescribed, but also with the duty of cleansing and lighting within the same. This Act laid the foundations of the modern system by concentrating under one body the whole business of watching, lighting, and cleansing. The city and suburbs were divided into 26 wards, each choosing one general and two resident Commissioners, besides which certain general Commissioners were nominated. The assessment was limited to 1s. 5d.

per £ of rent; the Superintendent of Police was made Procurator-Fiscal of Court; the Bailies were constituted Judges in cases occurring within, the Sheriff in those without, the royalty. Power was given to make bye-laws, and to regulate many matters such as tippling houses, brokers, hackney coaches, and coal-weighing. A Police Office was to be fixed for the convenience of the public where the Superintendent and Clerk were to be in attendance daily.

Amending Acts were passed in 1816 and 1817, but without introducing any important alteration on the general plan established in 1812. The benefit of the uniformity and centralisation was quickly felt in the unity and efficiency which they produced, and there was no attempt to revert to separate establishments. The old Town Guard was finally abolished in 1817.

The Act of 1812 was repealed in 1822 when certain improvements in the Police system were introduced, particularly by allowing a greater control to the ratepayers over the management and expenditure. The number of wards was increased to 30; authority was given to provide a Court Room, with cells for prisoners and accommodation for meetings and offices. In 1832 the Police bounds were further extended, and two other wards were added. For the year 1833-4, the total revenue was £29,331, and the expenditure £28,127.

The *Edinburgh Directory* for 1838 gives the

information that the Police establishment was located in Parliament Square; the Clerk was Mr John Thomson; and the General Commissioners were the following:—The Lord Provost, the four Bailies, Dean of Guild, Treasurer, and the Deacon Convener of the Trades, the Sheriff of the County and his Substitute, the first resident Bailie of Canongate, members chosen by the Faculty of Advocates, by the Society of Writers to the Signet, by the Company of Merchants, by the S.S.C. Society, and the Convener of the southern districts for the time being, together with 32 general and 64 resident Commissioners who were changed in November.

Further Acts were obtained, particularly in 1848, 1854, and 1856; and finally, after a process of evolution extending over a century the important Consolidation Act of 1879 was passed, which still continues to form the general basis for the Police administration of the city.

While the Commissioners were enlarging their offices and carrying on the statutory or police **The Present Constitution of the Council.** business of the community, the Town Council continued to discharge its functions in what is known as the municipal administration. The Reform Act of 1833 made an end of the old system of setts and close corporations, and transformed the Council into a properly representative body. The constitution of the Council since 1833 is well enough known, but can only be properly apprehended by keeping

The Sett of the Burgh

in view the two branches of local government, namely, the "municipal," which is the term applied to the Common Good and the administration under the Royal Charters and the Common Law; and the "police," which term is applied, not merely to the watching of the city, but to the whole statutory administration and finance of the Town Council.

Shortly after the Reform Act came into operation an elaborate Report on the Burghs of Scotland was drawn up for the information of the Government by a body called the Municipal Corporations Commission. In this Report the following passage occurred, which anticipated the course of events by which the Police Commissioners came to be merged with the Town Council:—

"We have made some inquiry into the practicability of merging the Police Board in the Town Council. In Edinburgh, as in all other burghs, the Town Council were the original managers of the police, as well as of the other common affairs of the town; and it was only when statutory assessments became necessary for purposes of police, that the inhabitants refused to place such powers in the hands of a body in whose appointment they had no voice. The town councillors are now, however, chosen by the same class of persons who elect the Commissioners of Police; and that objection being removed, it remained to inquire whether the duties of both offices were incompatible, or too laborious to admit of being discharged by the same individuals.

Municipal Corporations Committee

"The result of the evidence taken on this subject was, that a diligent commissioner of police may be employed in the duties of the office three or four hours a week, and there is reason to expect that the duty may in future become less laborious. Witnesses well qualified to judge of the matter were of opinion that the duties of both offices were compatible, and would not be too oppressive upon the persons on whom they should be imposed.

"It is difficult to find a sufficient number of fit persons willing to undertake the offices of town councillors and police commissioners, and it will therefore be a relief to the community to conjoin these. We are further of opinion that the Police Commission, as at present constituted, is considerably too numerous for efficiently discharging its duties.

"On the whole, after the maturest consideration, we have to recommend that the duties at present imposed upon the Commissioners of police in Edinburgh should in future be discharged by the Town Council, provided the municipal boundaries shall be extended, so that the councillors shall be elected by the whole body of persons who now vote in the election of police commissioners."

It may be added by way of supplement to this quotation that, although the reason for the distinction between municipal and police affairs in Edinburgh ceased to be valid after the Reform Act of 1833, the distinction nevertheless was continued for some considerable time, and was not abolished until 1856. In that year an important Act was passed "to extend the municipal boundaries of the City of Edinburgh, to transfer the powers of the Commissioners of Police to the Magistrates and Council and for other purposes." The Act extended the area of the city by including therein Canongate, Calton, Portsburgh and the area of the Police Commissioners, with the exception of a portion lying within the burgh of Leith which was disjoined from Edinburgh and annexed to Leith. Certain Acts relating to the Police Commissioners were repealed; their powers, property, and effects were transferred to the Town Council, and the municipal and police government and jurisdiction were united in the Town Council. It may be added by way of general statement that a public Act, called the Town Council Act, 1900, provided that throughout Scotland Town Councils should have and exercise the powers formerly possessed by Police Commissioners.

It will be recollected that under the old sett of the burgh the Town Council consisted of twenty-five members, and that in addition eight extraordinary deacons had rights of voting on certain occasions. The Act of 1833 provided that Edinburgh and certain other large towns should be divided into wards or districts which, together with the number of Councillors to be chosen by each ward or district, should be fixed and ascertained by Commissioners, named and appointed by His Majesty. These Commissioners divided the city into five wards, four of which were to elect six members each, and one of which was to elect seven members. This gave thirty-one members. The Act also provided that the Dean of Guild, elected by the guild brethren, and the Deacon Convener or Convener of Trades, elected by the convenery, should in virtue of their respective elections be constituent members of the Town Council, and should enjoy all the powers and perform all the functions which were then enjoyed or performed by them. With these additions the Town Council consisted of thirty-three members, this being the maximum number under the old sett. The Act provided that no distinction should be recognised between trades councillors and merchant councillors, and it made an end of the offices of Old Provost, Old Bailie, etc., and it transferred the election of the Dean of Guild from the Town Council to the Guildry.

The reformed Town Council thus consisted of the Lord Provost, four Bailies, Dean of Guild, Treasurer, Convener and twenty-five Councillors, and this number continued without alteration until the passing of the important Extension Act of 1856, already mentioned. This Act contained clauses providing that the Sheriff and another official should divide the city into thirteen wards for the purposes of parliamentary and municipal franchise, each ward to be numbered and to have a distinctive name. The number of persons to be elected as Councillors was thirty-nine, with the addition of the Dean of Guild and Convener of Trades as constituent members, making in all forty-one members; and the number of Magistrates was raised from four to seven, being the Lord Provost and six Bailies. In terms of this Act the wards were fixed as follows: (1) Calton, (2) Broughton, (3) St Bernard's, (4) St George's, (5) St Stephen's, (6) St Luke's, (7) St Andrew's, (8) Canongate, (9) St Giles', (10) St Cuthbert's, (11) George Square, (12) St Leonard's, (13) Newington.

On the passing of the Extension Act of 1896, which added Portobello and certain other areas to the city, the number of wards was increased to sixteen by the addition of (14) Portobello West Ward, (15) Portobello Middle Ward, and (16) Portobello East Ward. The Council was augmented by the addition of nine new members, making fifty in all. The number of Magistrates was fixed at eight, of whom the Lord Provost was one and seven were Bailies. Provision was also made for a redistribution of the wards of the city.

In 1900 the wards were re-arranged in accordance with an Act passed in that year which gives their boundaries in a schedule. They were then numbered and named as follows: (1) Calton, (2) Canongate, (3) Newington, (4) Morningside, (5) Merchiston, (6) Gorgie, (7) Haymarket, (8) St Bernard's, (9) Broughton, (10) St Stephen's, (11) St Andrew's, (12) St Giles', (13) Dalry, (14) George Square, (15) St Leonard's, (16) Portobello.

The Extension Act of 1920 added Leith and

the suburban districts to the area of the city. This Act provided that the added area should be divided into seven new wards, numbered and named as follows: (17) South Leith, (18) North Leith, (19) West Leith, (20) Central Leith, (21) Liberton, (22) Colinton, (23) Corstorphine and Cramond. The total number of elected Councillors was augmented to sixty-nine, making, with the Dean of Guild and Convener of Trades, seventy-one members in all. The number of Magistrates was increased to eleven, of whom the Lord Provost was one and ten were Bailies.

CHAPTER VIII

THE WORK OF THE TOWN COURTS

THE Royal Burgh of Edinburgh was from early times a favoured place. Privileges, the gift of many Kings, had procured for it a large amount of independence and self-government, cherished most zealously, although these were in most cases productive of much work to the men who governed it.

Although the population of Edinburgh cannot have been large, the bounds of the "liberties" were wide. They stretched from "the boundis of the fredome of Hadingtoun on the eist, quhilk is Egbuklingbray, and on the west to Almond watter, on the north to the sey, and on the south safar as the boundis of the serefdome of Edinburgh principall extendis to." Over this area the powers of the Town Council were considerable.

As in most other burghs, during a period of which the earliest date cannot be given but continuing till the Burgh Reform of the early nineteenth century, the Town Council may, in a manner, be separated from the actual community. The burgh was governed by an oligarchy, composed chiefly of members of the Merchant Guild, who year by year chose their own successors. It was not till after 1583 that the majority of the crafts obtained the recognition of their claim to be represented on the Council, and even then subject to restrictions. A study of the names of the members of the Council shows how, generation after generation, men of the same families governed the burgh. Nevertheless those who achieved and held that position had the responsibility for the government of the town, which was no light one, and, judging by the growth of the prosperity and importance of Edinburgh, they cannot have done it badly.

Apart from the Town or "Great" Council, as it is sometimes called, there were other Courts dealing with specialised branches of the Magistrates' duties. The composition of the earliest of these, the Guild and Burgh Courts, is nowhere exactly stated, but their members were also members of the Town Council. Of these the Burgh Court, the *Curia Capitalis Burgi de Edinburgh*, had the most extensive powers. By a Charter of King James III. in 1482 the Provost and Bailies were appointed Sheriff and Sheriffs-Depute of the Burgh, with both a civil and criminal jurisdiction. The Sheriff was judge in all crimes except treason, murder, fire-raising, robbery, and ravishment, with power however to try a murderer caught red-handed and a thief taken with the thing stolen in his possession, if proceedings were taken within three days. He was also judge in bloodwits, that is, fines for assault to the shedding of blood.

These powers gifted to the burgh were not

enjoyed by them without some controversy. The jurisdiction in matters criminal seems to have run counter to another jurisdiction, that of the Lord High Constable.

The powers of the Lord High Constable's Court extended to a certain radius round the King's person, given variously as twelve leagues, two leagues or four miles, known as the "Chamber of Peace." They also included the same distance from a meeting of Parliament in which the King was present, even only by his commission. This, it can be seen, might easily conflict with the rights of the Provost and Bailies of Edinburgh, and it is evident that to some extent it did so, although in the Cambridge MS., used by Miss Bateson in *The Scottish Kings' Household*, it seems as if it had been the intention to exclude the King's burgesses and other freemen from the jurisdiction of the Constable. These, " if accused of trespass within the verge, shall have his cross and borough market and shall be judged by his peers." In the first Protocol Book of the notary, John Foular, under the date 30th July 1501 is recorded an arrangement with the Earl of Errol, Lord High Constable, on the matter, in words which suggest that the Council conceived they were doing a favour to the noble Earl : " and als thai promittit to supple the said lord in his office of constabulari in tym to cum and nocht to be in his contrare in sic cais quhen it hapinis nor nain utheris concerning his office for his favor and kyndnes in tym to cum."

Agreements with the Constable

Among the Errol Papers, there is an obligation by the Provost, Bailies, and Council of Edinburgh of the 17th September 1507 to William, fourth Earl of Errol, narrating that he had constituted them and their successors "his deputs in the office of Constabularie for the term of three years next after the date hereof and thereafter for his will to endure." The Records of the Town Council show that this gift must have been prolonged, as the obligation suggests, for a note by the original transcriber of the first volume of the Acts of Council records that the Constable Court was held before the Provost and Bailies of the Burgh in 1511.

It was not of mere favour that the Constable consented to the deputing of his rights to the good town, as an entry of the 5th February 1520-21 shows, the Council then ordering that a payment to the Earl of Errol, promised for the office of Constabulary-Depute, amounting to 100 li., should be paid from the Common Good as the matter concerned the common welfare of the town.

Fortunately some evidence exists as the carrying out of these duties obtained from the Constable. Among the City Records there is a book containing the cases tried in the town for the months of June to September 1507 by the Bailies of the burgh, as representing three Courts: the *Curia Burgi*, or Burgh Court, the *Curia Vicecomitis*, or Sheriff Court, and the *Curia Constabularie*, or Constabulary Court. So far as can be seen from the few remaining pages of this record, in which some of the headings have been destroyed by damp, these three Courts were held sometimes together, sometimes separately, while the Bailies of the town invariably presided to the number of at least two. The only difference which marks the Courts and which tends to show that the office of Constable-Depute was not an empty name, is that cases of assault were, in the majority, tried by the *Curia Constabularie,* either alone or in conjunction with the other Courts.

The cases were for the most part far from serious, as one or two examples will show. "Distrublance," in modern language assault, really appears more ludicrous than serious after the lapse of four hundred years.

"1507. Jonet Fargusone convict be ane assis for the distrublance done till Jonet Dumfreis and drawing of hir blud for the quhilk caus scho wes adjuget to be seit upoun the gowf (pillory) quhill vj houris at evin nakit face and amerciament to the parti and that wes gevin for dome."

"Johnne of Crawfurd is convict be ane assis of the distrublance done till Marioun Broun the spous of Richert Dunlop and drawing of hir blud for the quhilk caus he wes adjugeit in amerciament of the court as he aucht to tyne upoun law and that wes gevin for dome.

"Marioun Broun convict be the said assis for the distrublance done till Johnne of Crawfurd and ruggin of his hair furth of his heid for the quhilk caus scho wes adjuget in amerciament of the court and amendis to the parti and that wes gevin for dome.

Agreements with the Constable

"Johnne of Crawfurd and Richert Dunlop ar fundin quit for the allegeit distrublance done ilk ane till uther."

Whatever the later connection of the Town with the Constable's Court, there are sufficient allusions scattered through the Council Records to prove that the Town's right of trying criminal cases was claimed and exercised, at least at intervals. The assessment of blood-wits is found frequently in the minutes of the Council, prefaced by an examination by surgeons of the Town as to the extent of the injury in question. One allusion to their rights is found in 1570, when an Act of Council mentions a claim by the Bailie of the Regality of Dalkeith for the release of three tenants of the regality, imprisoned in Edinburgh for assault on a mariner, committed on the high road to Leith. The Council rejected the claim, because the crime was committed inside their boundaries, and fell to be judged by them. Fifteen years later, on the occasion of the murder of Macmorane by one of the pupils of the High School, the Council sent a deputation to the King with reference to his interference with their privileges, in his postponing the Court. To be prevented from exercising the right to hold their Sheriff Court and punish a crime caught red-hand seems to have worried the Council almost more than the murder of the Bailie. But it was probably just as well, for the Magistrates were in no frame of mind to be anything but partial judges. After the notable tumult

The Work of the Town Courts

of the 17th December 1596, the King invited the Council to hold their court and try those guilty of the offence to His Majesty, but they wisely refused. Their situation was bad enough, without offending anyone else, as they were bound to do, either the King or the Kirk, both already incensed against the unfortunate Town.

Of the civil jurisdiction of the Magistrates there is an abundant record, for the Books of Decreets are unbroken from the year 1582 and chronicle the work of the Burgh Court, the *Curia Capitalis Burgi*, down to the present day. The powers of the Court seem to have been considerable in its early days, and it dealt with matters properly belonging to other courts. However, the importance of the cases tended to diminish rapidly, the matters out of its province were relegated to other courts, and it became merely a petty debt and petty offences Court. The regular business transacted included the service of heirs and retours of inquest, arrears of rent and annuals, evictions, recovery of debts, loans and pledges, and, rarely, minor thefts. Of the earliest matters treated, the Court Book of 1507, mentioned above, gives examples, notable because of their variety. These include a summons to the goldsmiths to produce a pageant, a proof that Edinburgh also had its elaborate religious processions.

" The quhilk day the baillies sittand in jugement chargit Patrik Forous, William Currour, Henry Yong, Alane Mosman, present, and all the laif of the

EDINBURGH CASTLE FROM THE SOUTH-EAST

goldsmithis in generale to forneis thair padgeant of
the passioun as thai wer wont for the plesour of our
soveraine lord and soveraine lady as thai sall ansuer
to the kingis grace and the provest thairupon."

Another entry illustrates the extent of Scots
trading ventures and the formalities of the time.

"The quhilk day M. Walter Layng desirit at
the baillies wald assigne a terme to David Child to
preif his writtingis producit in jugement obefor for
to pruf that thai wer selit with the seile of Tralsund
lauchfullie and lelelie with the avis of the consale
of the said toun of Tralsund."

An entry too long to be quoted narrates the
gift to Walter Chepman, the first Scots printer, of
an aisle in the Collegiate Kirk of St Giles, at the
back of St Anthony's Altar. The altar has vanished,
but the Chepman Aisle remains a monument to an
enterprising and very lovable man.

It would be easy to quote exhaustively from the
Burgh Court Books for the first fifty years, because
of the light thrown on sixteenth-century Edinburgh,
but extracts from the years 1581 to 1591 must suffice.

" Decernis and assolyeis queet in all tyme cuming
David Danielstoun fra the clame persewit be Adam
Dennum, goldsmith, aganis him acclamand ane ring
with ane fyne stane callit ane rubie ballet worthe
XII li. . . . quhilk the said Adam allegeit he laid
in wad to the said David of the sum of thrie pund
nynetein schillingis ane yeir syne or thairby in
respect of the said Davidis aithe thairupoun."

The Work of the Town Courts

An apprising at the instance of Nicol Uddert, merchant burgess, against Captain George Creich was for the sum of 200 li. on the following articles : "ane balhoille coffer coverit with blak leder, ane clok with slevis of blak grograme furrit with wolff skynis, ane clok with ane nek of blak serge lynit with talphetie, ane mandell of blak veluot of gascun fassoun pasmentit with blak pasmentis, ane pair of breikis of blak veluot with reid cordingis of silk and gold, ane uthare pair of breikis of violet veluot that ar awld, ane paire of hois of the myllane fassoun of gray veluot lynet with gray satyne and cannownes of gray satyn pikket owt, ane doublet of quhyt canves lynet with blew tapheteis and sewit with cordingis of gold, ane pair of gartenis of blew taphetie with pasmentis of gold, ane blak veluot bonnet without ane string, ane hat string of rowane silver and gold, sex buttouns of gold weyand ane unce and ane halff drop wrocht scharpe, with threttie sax buttouns of silver weyand ane unce and ane halff."

Uddert cannot have made what he expected from this apprising, for all this gay apparel only fetched 61 li. 17s. 10d.

How all sorts and conditions of men frequented Edinburgh is seen in the pages of this book : the brother of James VI.'s court favourite, the Earl of Arran, was sued for not paying his lodgings, and one of the troublesome family of the Tweedies of Drummelyier found the town a place to borrow ready money on the security of a gold chain of

fifty-seven links, for which he obtained 117 li. As
frequently, the lender did not get back the full value,
for the chain, being rouped, fetched only 104 li.

Another entry shows the extent of the jurisdiction
of the Court, for it records how Robert Nicolsoun,
candlemaker, sued Johne Fentoun, controller clerk,
and Robert Menteithe, *aide* in the King's petty
larder, for the breach of an agreement whereby he
should furnish nightly and every night for a month,
one and a half stone of candles for the King's house,
at 40s. for every stone, and that the contract should
be renewed after the first month.

A study of prices could be made from the Court
Books : some commodities were expensive, as the
following :—

"Decernis Allane Halbertsoun to content and
pay to William Littill, merchant, the sowme of ten
pund ten schillingis for certane schoit ribbenes coft
and ressavit be him fra the said Williame twelf oulkis
syne or thairby, in respect of the said W$^{mes.}$ aithe."

The Court also dealt with very domestic matters,
as in the account of how Issobell Legatt complained
that Marjorie Wricht had hired her five-footed
girdle for 8d. a day in 1587, and at that date, 1591,
had only returned the girdle a month ago, saying
that she was willing to pay if Issobell would repay
3 li. 7s. 8d. owing by her late husband, which she
protested had been paid already. Marjorie's oath
being taken, she was decerned quit of the claim.

Anything was good enough to apprise, from a

broadsword with a single guard to "ane womanis keming claithe of small linyng sewit with blak silk at all pairtis." Some things, however, fetched small prices, as "a painted bed of fir for 50s," "ane awld almery of aik" for 3 li. 16s., "ane pair of littill plaidis at 24s.," "fyve elnes of tiking of beddis" for 6s. the ell.

Surgeons also had recourse to this Court for payment of their fees: "Decernis Ester Loch and hir spous Eduard Loch to content and pay to David Hoppringill, chirurgeon, the sowme of ten merkis in compleitt payment and satisfactioun of his panes and travellis tane in curing and healing of the said Ester of ane diseas in hir leg and of ane uther diseas in hir bak, dew to the said David ane yeir syne or thairby, in respect of the said Esteris confessioun and modeficatioun of the baillie."

One other point may be noted, which is that in the earlier Court Books there are included cases belonging to the jurisdiction of the other courts, particularly of the Dean of Guild's Court. This is the more curious that the Guild Court was at least as early, if not earlier, than the Burgh Court. In 1507 there appear three cases of burgess-ships, and several neighbourhood cases, one of which concerns a Mosman, father or grandfather of the supporter of Queen Mary.

The exact position of the Dean of Guild and his Court, which was probably as old as the office, is difficult to define correctly. The Court, according to the *Statuta Gilde*, was composed of all members of the Guild, and probably was responsible for administering all their own affairs. But at what point and by what means the general jurisdiction of the Merchant Guild of Edinburgh became merged in or superseded by the Town Council there is no means of ascertaining. In Edinburgh the two were practically synonymous, although, in a somewhat perplexing manner, the Guild Court seems to have retained a separate identity. Lord Dean of Guild Millar, in his book *The Edinburgh Dean of Guild Court*, differentiates between the Guild Court and the Dean of Guild Court, characterising the latter as a committee of the former, "to which special business was assigned of a contentious character." But, even as a committee of the general Court, whose functions were exercised by the Town Council, it possessed a degree of independence not accorded to other committees, which placed it at once on a different footing. By an Act of Council of January 1500-1 it appears that the Provost, Bailies, and Council could control the meetings of the Guild Court, but in fact they never did, so far as is recorded. By an Act of Parliament of James IV. in 1503 it was ordained that the consent of the "great" Council was necessary for the making of burgesses, and that the dues received from them were to be considered a part of the Common Good and spent on the common works of the town : actually the Town Council only intervened in exceptional cases, and the money received by the Dean of Guild from that and other sources was earmarked for special purposes and recorded in separate accounts.

The composition of this court or council, for the word committee is never used of it, came under notice in the Decree Arbitral of James VI. in 1583, and in proceedings of the Town Council in the following year. By the decree the Dean of Guild was allowed to assemble "his brether and council in their gild courts comform to the ancient laws of the gildrie and privileges thereof." The council was further defined in the part of the decree dealing with the reception of burgesses and guild brethren as consisting of an equal number of merchants and craftsmen, not exceeding six persons. This was an innovation, as the earliest records of the Dean of Guild Court show. The *Neighbourhood Book*, in which the first entry is of the year 1529, shows that the composition of the Court varied, but included the Provost and Dean of Guild, sometimes two Bailies and the Treasurer, a number of Councillors, varying from two to five, and occasionally burgesses who were not of the Council. In January 1584-5, the Town Council, in terms of the Decree Arbitral, proceeded to the nomination of the Council of the Dean of Guild, and chose six persons, all councillors, though none were magistrates or office-bearers. In March of the same year the Town Council laid down the rules to govern the manner of their election and their powers. It was stipulated that members were to be men of good fame, known experience, care

Work of the Guild Council

and zeal for the common weal and guild brethren, and
that they must have served at least three years on
the Town Council. The wording and subsequent
practice seems to convey that they were not to be
members of the Town Council and Guild Council
simultaneously. The Dean of Guild of the past
year was also to be a member, and, though not
officially members, the Treasurer, Common Clerk,
and assessors were to be present at all meetings,
and "quhat baillies, counsallors or deykins sall pleis
to assist to be welcum to gif thair opiniouns."

Though the new regulations were approved and
passed, the regular working of the Guild Council
was delayed by a serious outbreak of pestilence in
the latter half of the year 1585, which was not
subdued till the beginning of the following year.
This and its consequences put all other matters
out of the heads of the Town Council, and as they
explained when the question was brought up again
in 1590 it had been "ouersene." But they ratified
the former Acts of Council and proceeded to elect
six members, none of whom were on the Town
Council. Thereafter the elections proceeded regularly,
fifteen days after the elections of the Town Council,
the members being neither magistrates, councillors,
nor deacons. The Guild Council or Dean of Guild
Court apparently was left to exercise its functions,
unchecked by any need to report to a higher
authority. Any interference was limited to rare
cases of neighbourhood, and of burgess-ships, guildries

or apprenticeships based on special circumstances. If, as suggested, the Guild Council were a committee, this proceeding was unusual, for all other committees had to report to the Town Council, as possessing no independent powers, and this placed it in an exceptional position, if indeed it does not point to some traces remaining of the jurisdiction of the early Guild Court.

The powers possessed by the Dean of Guild and his Court were carefully defined. They included the admission and booking of apprentices, burgesses, and guild brethren and the collection of their dues, the collection of the rents of booths in the neighbourhood of St Giles, the repair of the fabric of that church and of Trinity College Kirk, the provision of the elements for the sacrament and of linen cloths for the same, the registration of the cargoes of incoming and out-going ships, and the collection of their dues, the inspection of "neighbourhoods" and the supervision of weights and measures. For these matters he kept a separate account, in spite of the Act of Parliament mentioned above, allocating the dues of burgesses to the Common Good. The revenues of the Dean of Guild were, it is true, used for the Town's work, but never for other purposes than those assigned. Occasionally it happened that he had not sufficient money for repairs considered necessary by the Town Council, who seem to have retained the right of ordering pressing repairs, chiefly on the external fabric of the churches, and on the divisions

EDINBURGH CASTLE FROM THE EAST

made for the convenience either of the King or the Town. In such cases the deficit was met, not out of the Common Good, but from taxes levied for the purpose and accounted for by the Town Treasurer. The building of new churches also fell to the charge of the Town Treasurer. Apart from these church repairs, the revenue of the Dean of Guild was allotted to the duties of burgess-ships given each year to the Town Council and officers, to certain pensions, and to the rent and repairs of the ministers' houses.

The Act of Council, previously mentioned, of March 1584-5, recording the powers of the Dean of Guild and his Court, probably gave no new powers but served to explain their extent. In addition to control over the making of freemen, the Court had the right to punish unfreemen usurping the privileges of burgesses and to judge in disputes between burgesses. The control of shipping included the execution of all Acts of Parliament concerning the same. The right to collect dues from freemen included the right to levy "taxatioun" for the benefit of old and distressed members of the Guild, to enforce such taxes by means of fines and to appoint a treasurer for their collection.

The greater part of the work of the old Dean of Guild Court resembled the modern functions. It dealt with the amenity of the town, the supervision of buildings, according to regulations, and decisions regarding complaints between neighbours. The word "neighbourhood" is used to describe these cases,

The Work of the Town Courts

"neighbour" in the records of the period being used in the particular sense of freeman inhabitant of the burgh. The records of the court date back to 1529, at which time began the *Neighbourhood Book,* containing the judgments on such matters as were brought up for settlement by discontented inhabitants of the town. These include cases of encroachment in building, making windows overlooking adjoining property, possessing houses without chimneys, drainage, if indeed such a word can be applied to the prevailing lack of sanitation. We know that Edinburgh was supposed to be a dirty town— whether it was much worse than other great cities, such as Paris, is open to doubt. In fact, many scattered references dealt with dirt, middens, and other noisome things. But in justice to the old inhabitants of Edinburgh it should be stated that they were very particular about other people's unpleasant habits, and could complain in explicit and unvarnished terms as to the danger arising from their neglect of the common decencies of life.

The *Neighbourhood Book* is one which repays study. Besides the light thrown upon old inhabitants and closes, it shows the variety of cases which came under the jurisdiction of the Court and the care and apparent fairness of the decisions. A few examples may serve to illustrate the powers of the Dean and his Court, no matter how it was made up.

In 1532 the widow of John Vaus was found to have done no wrong in breaking out a window

opposite the garden of the Provost of St Giles,
provided she put in iron bars and glass. In 1538
a complaint made, that a house at the top of
Halkerston's Wynd was too high, was found to be
well founded. In 1540 Jonet Anderson was found
to have done wrong in "halding and feding geis
in the chalmers of the land pertening to hir . . . in
the Ovir Bow," having "rottin the same in ane pairt
therof." She also got into trouble for having a
"hairth" without a chimney, "becaus thair is na
passage quhairthrow the reik thairof may have
ascence bot abill to burn the haill hous gif ony fyre
beis usit thairin." In 1548 a case concerned the
right of entry to a close, when Katherine Lyntoun
and her husband were allowed free entry to the
"Byshop of Murrayes" close to gather up the tennis
balls from their court when people played there.
Apparently bad players were not unknown, and had
to be provided for. In 1554 John Rynd was found
to have done wrong in removing Issobell Maucham's
coat-of-arms from a carved stone at the Magdalene
Chapel. He was ordered to have the stone recut
at his own expense. In 1556 a maltman was accused
of "steiking up of the fute of the clois callit Crammys
clois and using thairof as ane hous and causing
thairby filth to stand in the fute of the said clois
towart the Cowgait." This entry gives the prevailing
idea of drainage—that everything was all right if
only the dirt went somewhere else. One wonders
where it went in the Cowgate! The following,

The Work of the Town Courts

according to modern standards, is unpleasantly vague: "ordanis in all tyme cuming that na muk or fulyie (filth) be laid in Diksouns wynd . . . langer nor the accustomat tyme." In 1569 a complaint was made that certain lands in Peebles Wynd were so ruinous that the adjoining lands belonging to the wife of an influential burgess, Mr Michael Chisholme, were in danger. The vaults had fallen down during the preceding night and she expected not only the destruction of her land but also that of her children and household. If it were so pressing a danger, why, one wonders again, did they not flit the household! In 1577 the Dean of Guild and his Court assembled on the ground of a maltman outside the West Port, granted him permission to lay flagstones over the gutter in front of his house, provided that he did not block the ordinary passage of water. One last entry, because it throws light on the kind of buildings which at one time lined the High Street, of which one bit remains in a milk-shop in the Lawnmarket. In 1599 Andrew Stevinsoun was allowed to build his waste land on the north side of the street "ather be rainge pillar or massie wark as he pleissis . . . and to have na hingand staires without the same." One hopes that the worthy Andrew chose the "rainge pillar," for the burgh would indeed have been handsome if a long arcade did run the length of the whole High Street. But that and many other results of the Dean of Guild's judgments no one will ever know.

CHAPTER IX

THE OLD CITY DEBT

AT an early stage in their history the Scottish burghs were provided with a code of law and put under the care of one of the great officers of State, the Lord Chamberlain, who visited the burghs to ingather the dues of the Crown, and among other things to inquire whether "faithful compt" was made of the Common Good. The duty of rendering an annual account was enforced on the burghs by various Acts of Parliament, certain of which narrate that for lack of such accounting Royal Burghs, by the maladministration of their Magistrates, had fallen under great debts and burdens. Whether the accounting was at any period duly made, and how far it was effective to control the actings of the Town Councils may be doubtful, but in any case it appears that after the Union of the Crowns this salutary regulation by degrees fell into abeyance. In succeeding years it became apparent that it was unwise to leave Magistrates free to act without check or control, as a consequence of which the finances of many burghs fell into a state of confusion. Lord Kames in one of his sketches wrote that in his day the revenues of a royal burgh were seldom laid out for the good of the town, but in making friends to the party who were in possession of the Magistracy and in rioting and drunkenness for which every pretence was laid hold of, particularly that of hospitality to strangers. "Such mismanagement tends to idleness and corruption of manners which accordingly are remarkable in most royal burghs. Another consequence no less fatal is the strong desire in every licentious burgess of stepping into the magistracy for his own sake and that of his friends; hence the factions and animosities that prevail in almost all the royal burghs which are violently and indecently pursued without the least regard to the good of the community." No towns are named in this serious indictment, but it may reasonably be surmised that Lord Kames had in view the case of Edinburgh, which was made the victim of denunciation almost as emphatic by other writers, including Lord Cockburn. It is unfortunate that the age which gave us the new town of Edinburgh and the docks of Leith should be exposed to such grave criticism.

Any narrative which proposed to explain how the old city debt developed from stage to stage **Rise of the Debt.** would bring up the general history of Edinburgh. While this cannot be attempted it may be of interest to give a few particulars regarding the rise of the debt.

Royal Borrowings

Previous to the era of the Reformation and the reign of King James VI., the burgh doubtless had its troubles, being sometimes involved in civic disorder, at other times affected by invasions from England; but it seems at least to have kept out of debt. When the Roman ritual was cleared out the Town Council appropriated much of the property of that church, not only in silver and gold but in houses and lands. It may be said that the Council took advantage of the embarrassments of Queen Mary, but the position was entirely different with her son, King James, who made his state of poverty a constant pretext for exactions from the town. When, for example, the marriage of the King was being negotiated with the Princess of Denmark, the Town Council were required to fit out a ship to bring him home with his wife at a cost of £500 scots per month; and they were also necessitated to pay £40,000 scots as part of the dowry of the Queen. The sum was so enormous that the burgh was obliged to borrow the money at ten per cent. interest. This is probably one of the first instances of what is familiar to everyone now as borrowing on capital account; and it may with tolerable safety be accepted as the germ of the old city debt.

If the needs of King James were great, it is certain that the needs of King Charles I. were greater, and his attacks on the town funds were frequent and serious. In 1626 the Town Council, ever willing to serve the Stuarts, contributed £60,000 to the King; the visit of the King three years later added another sum of £41,000; another visit brought forth £12,000; and immediately afterwards the town expended £60,000 for sending forces into England to assist the Parliament. In 1638 the debt of the city is said to have amounted to £151,000 scots. The distress to which the burgh was reduced at this period seems to have banished virtue from the Town Council altogether, for they refused either to pay interest or capital to the lenders until compelled to do so by the tribunals set up by Cromwell. In 1658, during Cromwell's domination, the city debt amounted to £550,000 scots; and two years later, at the Restoration of the monarchy, it amounted to £792,921 scots. In order to raise revenue the Town Council received a grant for a number of years of certain duties on ale, wine and spirits, but, although the citizens had now to pay for the extravagance of their rulers, there came no sign of retrenchment or reform.

It might be natural to inquire how such things were permitted. The answer might be that the Corporation was self-elected and did not represent the citizens; that the burgh was dependent on favours from those in positions of authority; and that in those times there was neither regular law nor justice. There indeed prevailed everywhere a general prostration of public feeling and a state of corruption throughout the whole of public life.

Purchase of Favours

In Maitland's history mention is made of the pension paid by the Royal Burghs to the Duke of Lauderdale in 1661 and of a payment of £3600 scots made to him by the Magistrates of Edinburgh in order to ingratiate themselves with this brutal minister. A few years later, in return for the grant of certain imposts on wine, they paid him £6000. They also paid him the enormous price of £6000 sterling for what was called the town of Charlestown, but is more familiar to us by the name of the Citadel in Leith. This was done, as Maitland says, "to prevent their falling under the displeasure of this mighty prime minister." Similar incidents might be quoted concerning the Earl of Middleton, who also was one of the favourites of Charles II., and Viscount Melfort, Secretary of State to King James VII. After the transfer of the Court to London, the Town Council found it convenient to negotiate their business there by means of suitable agents, who appear to have shared the rapacity of those with whom they transacted the affairs of the town. One of the Town Clerks, by name John Hay, was sent to London nineteen times at vast expense. Other Town Clerks, who were even more notorious, were Thomson and Rocheid; the former on one occasion was "gratified" by the present of £1000; and the latter received £3337 sterling, as his share in certain Court transactions. Up to the period of 1680 the Corporation of Edinburgh spent large sums in the purchasing of grants, the chief purpose of which was to tax the inhabitants. It has been said that until this period the funds of the city were plundered and the city debt created by flagitious princes, courtiers and officials; but this of course does not exonerate the Town Council.

In the year 1718 it is stated in the Sederunt Book of the Town Council that the amount of the city debt was £25,418 sterling, but it is difficult to believe that this figure can be correct. Thereafter a new element appeared and served to complicate matters. This was the creation of a separate and distinct debt, arising from money borrowed on the security of a tax called the "Ale and Beer Duty." The debts existing in 1718 were transferred to this account, and upon this security further sums were borrowed for "meliorations" whereby the city debt was increased within a few years to £73,414. It has been mentioned that a tax was granted on ale and wine enduring for a limited time. In 1693 a new impost was obtained because of the exigencies of the town, the amount being two pence scots on every pint of ale or beer, to be exacted during a limited number of years. The tax was renewed from time to time and did not expire finally until 1837. The complications after 1718 arose from the fact that, owing to the system of book-keeping, there seem to have been two revenues, two exchequers, and two debts. There was also a third classification at a later date, namely the accounts of the harbour and docks of Leith.

A Review of the Debts

Bailie Smith and other Critics.

When Adam Black was City Treasurer he published a pamphlet entitled a *View of the Financial Affairs of the City of Edinburgh*. In this pamphlet he refers to the debt of the city in the year 1658, and states that the town had then great difficulty in paying its way and had continued to be in difficulties down to his day. He also states that, in order to enable the citizens to discharge their grievous burden, the tax known as the ale duty had been granted by Cromwell for a term of eleven years, but this duty failed in its object and the city debt, instead of disappearing, continued to increase so that it was found necessary to renew this tax from time to time. According to Hugo Arnot, the city debt had increased to £78,164 in 1723, and by a Statute of that year extending the ale duty the Magistrates were authorised to borrow a further sum not exceeding £25,000, but were prohibited from ever increasing the city debt by more than this amount, and for the debts the ale duty was answerable in the first place, and the other funds of the city subsidiary. Fortunately or otherwise the prohibition contained in this Act was never enforced. Hugo Arnot, writing in 1779, gives the figures of the ale duty, the produce of which fell from £8000 in the year 1724 to £2197 in the year 1776. The explanation he gives of this fall, which put the Magistrates entirely out of their reckoning, is certainly an odd one. He says that the people stopped drinking ale, and instead thereof took to consuming tea and whisky, thus defeating the tax; and these two habits are combined by him as propagating "idleness, vice and disease" among the people. "The Magistrates borrowed money upon the faith of this revenue to enable them to carry out works of public utility. Much obloquy and unmerited censure have been thrown upon the administration of the city, particularly upon the public-spirited and excellent magistrate George Drummond for thus anticipating the city revenues as if it had been possible for them to have foreseen and conceived so amazing a decrease in a duty arising from one of the most necessary articles of life." He adds that in 1779 the city debts were less by about £8000 than in 1723, being £70,195, the explanation being the sales of certain properties; that the administration of the city funds appears of late to have been excellent, more especially when it is considered that the purchase of lands, building of the North Bridge, making sewers, paving streets and other expenses of the extended royalty amounted in 1778 to £37,354.

A less complacent view was expressed by Thomas Smith, one of the Old Bailies, who delivered an address from his place at the Council table on 27th September 1799, at the choosing of leets for the new Magistrates. He spoke like an oracle, and his address, being printed and put into circulation, fell upon the citizens as the first definite warning of the evil to come. A perfect flood of pamphlets followed, this being the form, imported from revolutionary France, in which the political controversies of the time were waged. Bailie Smith was a banker and financier who had entered the Town Council in 1795. He was impressed with the large money transactions going on, large sums being borrowed upon bond and promissory note, large sums being taken in upon life annuities, with large warrants of expenditure and large balances due to bankers, as reported to the Council every week. He made inquiry among his colleagues whether the city kept any books, and they answered that they did not know, excepting that the Chamberlain's Cash Book was laid every Wednesday upon the Council table. "This book I have often looked into, but I never understood it, and I have the authority of the present Chamberlain for saying that it is not intended to be understood by every member of Council." The Chamberlain's office dates from 1766 and was then filled by Mr Hugh Buchan upon an appointment renewed annually. Mr Buchan retired in 1796 and was succeeded by Mr Thomas Hay. "At the period when Mr Hay came into office, I met him by accident in North Frederick Street and talked a little of his appointment. He said he was sorry to acquaint me the town's affairs appeared to him to be in very bad order. I answered I was sorry to hear it, inquiring how they stood. He replied he did not know their actual situation. I asked who knew then, receiving nothing in answer but a very significant shrug of his shoulders. 'What!' said I, 'does the Lord Provost not know?' 'He does not.' 'The Town Clerk?' 'He does not.' 'Then Mr Buchan must surely know?' 'Mr Buchan knows nothing of the matter.' I was thunderstruck at the information that a gentleman who had been for thirty years Chamberlain of the city, having the whole revenue and expenditure passing through his hands, was unable to give satisfactory information on the state of the town's affairs. I never afterwards thought it surprising that the same thing should appear in any member of the Council."

Bailie Smith mentions two motions submitted by him to the Town Council. One of these urged the need for economy and asked that an instruction be given to the new office-bearers to direct their exertions and attention towards this end. This was negatived by the Council. The other proposed that there be no election dinner at the expense of the city, which would save the good town from £100 to £150; this also was negatived on the ground that the dinner had been already bespoke.

In the Address it is stated that the city possessed no ledgers, and that the same mode of book-keeping was followed which had been in use for a hundred years. The Town Clerk disapproved of any change as throwing what he conceived to be a stigma on his old friend the Chamberlain. The money required to meet the interest on the city debt was borrowed from the bank; there were no sinking funds; no rental existed, showing the feu-duties belonging to the Corporation, and the collection of the city revenues showed increasing arrears. "The system of management will require to be greatly altered, indeed, economy must not only be introduced into every department, but rigidly enforced, regular books ought to be kept open to the inspection of every member of Council, no expenditure ought to be authorised unless there be a fund to answer it. Above all, a Sinking Fund ought to be introduced, and if these things shall not be attended to, I hesitate not to say that ere long the administration of the city's affairs will go from under the Magistrates and be placed in the hands of Trustees."

Bailie Smith made out various accounts showing the financial position so far as he could ascertain it. According to his figures the city debt amounted in 1751 to £71,997; in 1798 it amounted to £168,982. For the ten years ending Martinmas 1795 the ordinary revenue of the city was £300,384; and the ordinary expenditure was £303,719. In the same period the debt of the city had increased by £63,781. He made certain categoric accusations against the financial system: firstly, that the city revenue was not rendered as efficient and productive as it might be by good and proper management; secondly, that the expenditure was not conducted with as much economy as it might be; thirdly, that the capital debt, contrary to the statements of the Magistrates, was increasing rapidly.

An answer to Mr Smith's address was published by authority of the Town Council, giving a different version of the City Accounts. The reformer lost his seat in the Council, and was subjected to much public persecution. He was accused of endeavouring to ruin the credit of the city and thereby to embarrass and obstruct the measures of the Town Council; nothing less than a solemn recantation could heal the wound given to the finances of the town, and the grief, misery, and distress occasioned by his pamphlet to those who had placed their funds with the Corporation. "The present Magistrates have no occasion to excuse themselves either on account of the amount of the City's debt or for the manner in which the books are kept."

Passing from Bailie Smith and his address, it should be mentioned that the affairs of Edinburgh were frequently brought before Parliament in the early years of the last century. They were the subject of examination by a Committee of the House of Commons in 1819, when statements and returns were made by the City Accountant and Chamberlain. This Committee reported that from 1807 to 1816 the amount of the sums borrowed and raised by way of annuity, and received for property sold, had exceeded the amount of debts paid off and of sums paid for property purchased by £90,421; and that the excess of expenditure over income during the two following years amounted to £16,000 and £18,000.

The report of this Committee also dealt with the grievances of burgesses in Scotland, and referred to the lack of any control by them over the expenditure of burgh funds or the contraction of debt; and the want of any power to call upon the Magistrates to account for their intromissions. In their investigations in Edinburgh they took evidence from Lord Provost Kincaid M'Kenzie, the Dean of Guild, the City Chamberlain, the Town Clerk, "and various other persons who have at different times been members of the council, and they all profess to have been themselves and all their colleagues wholly uninformed of the actual situation of the city's pecuniary affairs; and all state that the books kept were not such as to afford the requisite information, and that at no time was any statement of its affairs laid before the council or any inquiry instituted. . . . It appears from the Lord Provost's evidence that during the last 18 months a series of motions and protests in succession were made by Deacon Paterson and others, but no statement was laid before the council; for which the lord provost has in evidence assigned as a reason that he did not consider it his duty merely to gratify Deacon Paterson."

The subject likewise came under the consideration of the Commissioners on Municipal Corporations in 1833. As a result of their investigations this

The Old City Debt

Commission reported that from an early period the Magistrates had made alienations of the common land of the burgh to assist their revenues and in return for annual payments which were merely nominal. Fortunately for the town the extreme sterility of that part of their property called the Burgh Loch and marsh was such as to save it from feuing until at a later period it had been drained and converted into productive soil. The report described the state of the city affairs as disastrous. "We have not found sufficient evidence to entitle us to report that the disastrous state of the city affairs has been caused by actual embezzlement or fraudulent malversation. Exaggerated expectations of the continued and indefinite increase of the city in prosperity and size may have led the Managers of the Corporation into an increase of expense far disproportioned to the really considerable growth of the revenue ; officers were multiplied and salaries raised ; a spirit of litigation prevailed, great profusion took place in the expenses of civic parade and entertainments, and extravagant sums were expended on public buildings and other works, as ill adapted in general to their object of embellishing the city, as they invariably were disproportioned to its expenses. The expense of law proceedings for the city for the period from 1819 to 1832 was £24,162; for the year 1819 the cost of city entertainments was £782; in 1820, £1066; and the election dinner of the Magistrates that year cost

The Harbour of Leith

£533. . . . . The closeness and irresponsibility of the
Corporation could not alone account for the con-
tinuance of such a system; the studied concealment
of the affairs of the community for a long period,
and the partial and confused statement of them
which was afterwards periodically made, probably
kept the respectable members of the Corporation
in ignorance of their financial embarrassment, and
it is that ignorance and reckless confidence in the
future improvement of their finances which can
alone save the city managers from the charge of
fraud both as regards the community and their
creditors."

The Harbour of Leith was confirmed to the city
by a Charter of King Robert the Bruce in 1329,
Leith Harbour and for 500 years thereafter the Town
and Docks. Council of Edinburgh were responsible
for managing this undertaking. Leith was for long
a small port with a dry and inconvenient harbour,
but in the early years of last century it became
possessed of the East and West Docks, and thus
of accommodation not surpassed by many seaport
towns. On the site of these docks and their quays
and warehouses and even over what is now Commercial Street the sea used to ebb and flow. We
may therefore judge of the enormous expense
which must have been incurred in constructing
these massive works, and this chapter of the old
city debt requires to be considered by itself.

The Corporation obtained at different times

statutory powers to carry out these improvements and to borrow the necessary monies. Put shortly, it came to this, that in 1799 power was given to borrow £80,000; in 1805, power was given to raise another sum of £80,000; and in 1813, power was given to raise a third amount of £80,000. In 1805, the Lords of the Treasury were authorised to advance £25,000 to the Corporation of Edinburgh upon an assignment of the rates of the harbour and docks, "and all the estate, right, title and interest of the said Lord Provost, Magistrates and Council in and to the same, and all quays, houses, lands or other property purchased for the purposes of the said harbour, basins, docks and other works." Thus in 1813 the debt on the harbour, due to individuals, was £240,000, and to the Government £25,000.

But the plans of the city, however well conceived and beneficial in the long run, were far from satisfactory to the people of Leith. Tradition often gives a confused version of history, and in the case of Leith it is popularly supposed that the struggle between the port and the city was from first to last a war of independence.

That aspect of the old rivalry came into prominence in 1896, when amalgamation was then attempted by the city; but at an earlier date when Town Councils throughout Scotland were close corporations, unrepresentative and irresponsible, Leith probably was more concerned about trading grievances, about the exclusive rights claimed by

Conditions at the Docks

Edinburgh as a royal burgh, and the administration of the harbour, which operated against the interests of its merchants. Thus, when the Leith Police Bill of 1827 was being promoted, it was stated that the "chief ground of division and contention betwixt Edinburgh and Leith of late years has been the proceedings of the former with respect to the harbour and docks. These proceedings have been of such a character as to call forth repeatedly within the last 40 years the determined opposition of the inhabitants of Leith." The streets at the docks were ill paved and worse lighted, goods were stolen by the cart load; upwards of forty people were drowned in the harbour within four years for want of a few chains and lamps; the port charges were multiplied so that ships avoided Leith. In many instances charter-parties provided against delivery at Leith unless on payment of an additional freight. "Vessels have gone to the port of Fisherrow, about six miles distant, and there discharged their cargoes which were sent by cart to Edinburgh, and notwithstanding the additional expense they find it a cheaper mode than to discharge at Leith. Cargoes of wood have been landed at Grangemouth and brought into Edinburgh by the Union Canal to save the port charges."

In 1825, the Corporation endeavoured to transfer the docks to a Joint Stock Company, and brought a Bill into Parliament, which was stoutly opposed by the people of Leith, and failed. The purchase price was fixed at £300,000 ; the members of Council and their friends acquired part of the shares and jobbed in the stock ; and at the end of the day their expenses came out of the Common Good.

After this failure a transaction was entered into between the Corporation and the Government, by which the Government obtained certain parts of the docks for the use of the Navy, and the Treasury were authorised to advance £240,000, thus taking over the whole of the dock debt which stood at £265,000. The harbour and docks, with all the rates and duties accruing to them, were transferred by way of security to the Barons of Exchequer. In 1826, an Act of Parliament vested the management of the harbour and docks in statutory commissioners "in consequence of numerous disputes with ship-owners and merchants and of large loans made by Government as well as for the purpose of making further improvements and adopting a more effective system of management." The number of commissioners was twenty-one, elected by the Corporation and certain public bodies. But while the power of maintaining and improving the harbour was vested in the new body, the Corporation retained the right to the revenue and therefore to fix the rates, and they also appointed the revenue officers and the clerk. The new régime failed to abate the strife which existed between the merchants of Leith and the Corporation, as the dock rates continued to be imposed and levied with a view to obtaining a surplus which might be applied towards the general and pressing purposes of the city. This was a rock of offence; to the people of Leith the idea of a profit being made out of the industry of the inhabitants of a commercial community by the inhabitants of another town and a different community was preposterous.

On 28th August 1833 the Burgh Reform Act became law, and on the day following an Act was **The City Creditors.** passed appointing Trustees for the creditors of the City of Edinburgh. The Act proceeds on a long preamble which states the position of the Government in relation to the harbour and docks of Leith, and continues in these words—"And Whereas large debts have been contracted and are still owing by the City of Edinburgh to various other creditors, and it is desirable that measures should be taken for a speedy reduction and settlement of the debts of the said city in so far as there are or may be funds legally available for that purpose and for the security of the Creditors, and in the meantime to prevent undue preferences among the Creditors, and to save the expense which Creditors may incur by competing among themselves, or by doing legal diligence for the recovery of their debts. . . . Be it enacted that the right honourable Sir William Rae of Eskgrove, Baronet, Sir James Gibson Craig of Riccarton, Baronet, John Bonar of Ratho, Banker, Richard Mackenzie of Dolphinton, deputy-keeper of H.M. Signet, William MacHutcheon, Merchant in Edinburgh, and John Learmonth, present Lord Provost of the City of Edinburgh shall be and are hereby nominated and appointed Trustees for the said Creditors, for the purpose of realising and distributing among the said Creditors in the most expeditious and economical manner the whole estate and effects heritable and moveable, real and personal, wheresoever situate and of whatever denomination belonging to the said city, which are legally liable for the said debts and attachable by the diligence of the said Creditors." The estates and effects of the city were vested in the Trustees to the end that they might be levied, recovered, sold and converted into money for the benefit of the Creditors, but the Town Council were not to be divested of any estate or effects not liable for debts nor attachable by diligence. An exception was also made of the harbour and docks of Leith, conveyed to the Government in security of their advances. Until the rights of the Town Council and the Trustees were ascertained, the revenue of the city was to be collected by the City Chamberlain, and so much thereof was to be applied as might be required to enable the Town Council to defray the annual expenditure of the city, this amount to be fixed by the Court in default of agreement. The Trustees had power to sell, feu and lease, to grant bonds, to carry on actions, to compromise debts; and the Trust was to come to an end

with consent of the Treasury and four-fifths in value
of the Creditors.

This Act gave rise to a series of important and
difficult questions between the Creditors and the
Magistrates as to the nature of the obligations
implied in the gift of common property to a burgh,
and as to the portion thereof which could be attached
for its debts. These disputes formed the subject of
suits at law, and some of them were never resolved.
For example, the Trustees claimed to be entitled
to appropriate the seat rents of the city churches,
but this claim brought forward the Kirk-Sessions
and led to the well-known case of Clapperton *versus*
the City, which was defended at first by the Trustees
and at a later stage was abandoned by them and
thereafter litigated with the Town Council. Considerable sums were advanced from time to time
to the Magistrates to enable them to meet the
municipal expenses without any definite arrangement
being made. Again Leith became a Parliamentary
Burgh in 1833 with a Town Council of its own,
but the new local authority had no revenue or
Common Good to enable it to function properly,
and Edinburgh was not in a position to hand over
the produce of the Petty Customs of the port
estimated to amount to £500 a year. It was,
however, contended that the primary purpose for
which these customs were levied was to uphold the
municipal establishment, and this question was
obviously a vital one for Leith. The sederunt books

The Old City Debt

and papers recording the meetings and actings of
the Trustees for the Creditors are stored in the City
Chambers, but it is not possible to give any adequate
statement of their contents in a short article. The
position taken up by the Creditors was, of course,
that they should be paid in full, and various propositions made for a settlement by compromise were
rejected.

The debts due to creditors other than the
Government, including the sums secured on the ale
Reports and duty, amounted in round figures to
Proposals. £400,000. The government debt was
about £236,000. The rate of interest current on
first-class investments at the time was about 4
per cent. The annual revenue of the city was
stated to be £22,000 but this included a doubtful item of £7000 for seat rents from the city
churches. The sum claimed as actually necessary
for civic expenditure was £11,000, but the Creditors
did not assent to this appropriation, and contended
that even £7000 was excessive for this purpose, and
that the amount should be limited to the produce
of the Common Good or Petty Customs, this being
about £4720. With the City Accounts in a state
of confusion, and every item uncertain, calculations
differed and figures could be made, and were made,
to support widely different propositions. If the seat
rents and other debatable items were omitted the
annual remainder was sufficient to yield the Creditors
$1\frac{1}{3}$ per cent. on their debts. Other views brought

out 2 per cent., 2½ per cent., 3 per cent., even 4⅓ per cent.

In 1835 Adam Black was City Treasurer and he published a pamphlet entitled a "View of the Financial Affairs of the City with Suggestions for a Compromise with the Creditors." He deprecated the litigations being carried on to ascertain the rights of parties, the only result of which was the annual destruction of £4000 to £5000 of the property belonging either to the City or the Creditors for as many years as the lawsuits might last. He justified the exaction of seat rents and dock dues, and was alarmed at the possibility of any new assessment being put on the citizens. Such a power was not then possessed by the Town Council; "but the City is already overburdened by so many heavy impositions that an addition to our assessments in the present languishing state of the town would be disastrous; strangers are already deterred from settling among us because Edinburgh is one of the heaviest taxed towns in the Empire." He scoffed at the pretensions of Leith. "Supposing it should be acknowledged that for five centuries the affairs of Leith under the direction of Edinburgh have been oppressively and prodigally conducted, the harbour was as much the property of the Corporation of Edinburgh as the harbour of Cockenzie is the property of Mr Cadell; and the inhabitants who congregated around it had no more peculiar right to it than the increasing inhabitants of Cockenzie may on some future day have to Mr Cadell's harbour, or to insist on a count and reckoning as to the moneys expended on the port and the revenues derived from it. It is something like delusion on the part of the individuals who happen at present to reside in Leith to complain of the damage sustained by the oppressive and injurious conduct of the superiors of the harbour. . . . There is not the most distant probability of the Crown violating engagements with other parties in order to favour the town of Leith." Treasurer Black's proposal was that the Creditors should receive 2½ per cent. interest on their debts, and his figures allowed also for an annual Sinking Fund payment of £2776. Nothing, however, came of his proposal.

In the year 1835 a Select Committee of the House of Commons investigated the affairs of Edinburgh. The existence of the government debt was perhaps a factor of advantage to the city, and one of the few points upon which the Town Council and the Trustees were united was in the desire that the government should stand aside and allow a preference to be given to the ordinary creditors. The Select Committee brought in a report on which, as it happened, no definite proposal was made to the Creditors. The following passage occurs in this report: "Your Committee have come to the conclusion that they are justified in recommending to Parliament to abandon or suspend, either wholly or in part, the debt now due to Government from the Corporation, provided that adequate public objects can be accomplished by this remission. It appears to them, however, that it is impossible to entertain any hope of effecting such objects unless the other parties interested shall approach the proposed arrangement in a spirit of mutual sacrifice and concession. The points of the greatest consequence to secure, appear to your Committee to be to limit the claims of the Creditors of the City, and to effect a composition of their amount upon fair and equitable terms; to dissever the connection which at present exists between Leith and Edinburgh, and to vest the property and management of the port in Commissioners under suitable regulations which could provide for its maintenance and improvement; and especially to relieve its trade from the payment of the merk per ton, upon adequate compensation being secured to those who were entitled to it."

In January 1836, a Report regarding the city and Leith was prepared by Henry Labouchere, Vice-President of the Board of Trade, afterwards Lord Taunton. This Report went into elaborate detail; was widely circulated, and, to judge by the numerous prints published against it, the proposals it contained pleased no one. Amongst other "observations" put forward in the Report were the following: (1) that the Government should give up one half of its debt and postpone the remainder without interest ; (2) that the Creditors should make a deduction of 25 per cent. from the amount of their debts and accept 3 per cent. bonds for the remainder ; (3) that the payment of the interest to the Creditors should be secured by an assessment on the inhabitants ; (4) that the management of the harbour and docks should be vested in a new body of commissioners independent of and unconnected with the Town Councils of Edinburgh and Leith. In the Report the free revenue from Leith Docks was stated at £14,000, from which it was proposed to pay £6000 to the city, whereof part should be applicable to the ministers, the college and schools, and part for other civic purposes. This proposal, so far as the Creditors were concerned, meant that they should receive £9000 per year on debts reduced from £400,000 to £300,000. This was at once rejected by the Trustees and also disapproved by their constituents.

In July 1836 the Select Committee of the House of Commons proposed that the Creditors should receive $3\frac{1}{4}$ per cent. on three-fourths of their debts, or £9750 per year ; and they also proposed to increase the allowance from the Leith revenues to £7000, of which £2500 was to be applicable for civic purposes including the payment of interest to Creditors. This proposal was likewise rejected by the Trustees for the Creditors.

At a later stage negotiations were opened up between the Trustees and the Town Council, in the

Attempts at Settlement

course of which the latter, with the approbation of the Chancellor of the Exchequer, proposed to allow the Creditors 4 per cent. on three-fourths of their debts, or £12,000 of yearly interest, and to apply an additional sum of £2000 per year towards a Sinking Fund. In this way the city would have become bound to pay £14,000 yearly until the debt was extinguished and this payment was to be guaranteed by a power of assessment. This offer having been sanctioned by the Trustees, was submitted to a meeting of the Creditors, when it was strenuously opposed by Colonel Macdonald of Powderhall and certain other influential individuals, and finally rejected, since it failed to secure the four-fifths majority required by the Act. The rejection led to the retirement from the Trust of the Earl of Rosebery, Lord Viscount Melville, Sir James Gibson-Craig, and Mr Richard Mackenzie, all of whom had advised the Creditors to accept the offer.

Negotiations and Agreement.

The attempts to effect a settlement by a fixed composition on the amount of the city debts having failed, an endeavour was then made to determine the properties and revenues which were considered to be liable for debts, as distinguished from those liable only for current municipal expenses. This also failed, but it produced from the Creditors an offer to accept an annuity of 3 per cent. on their debts secured over the whole funds of the Corporation.

247

The Old City Debt

Some delay followed, but on 6th December 1837 an Agreement was reached for a general settlement on the principle of a limited security. The subject of this Agreement was described by the City Treasurer as perhaps the most important which ever came under the consideration of the Town Council. The Agreement provided for the issue to the Creditors of bonds bearing 3 per cent. interest to cover the whole amount of their debts and to be redeemable at par. The bonds were secured over certain specified revenues and properties of the Corporation, but the market customs and other items of the Common Good were excluded from the security except to the extent of £1000, which was allowed in respect of certain properties to which the Creditors alleged a claim. On the assumption that the debt amounted to £400,000, the annual interest payable to the Creditors would have been £12,000; the actual debt, however, was fixed and ascertained at £385,035. No provision was made for a Sinking Fund or a special assessment for the benefit of the Creditors, but at the moment there were indications that the revenues of the Corporation were improving. In 1838 a penny rate would have brought in about £1350.

In the negotiations Sir William Rae's name was prominent on the side of the Creditors; on the other side the leading personages were the City Treasurer, Duncan M'Laren, and the Solicitor-General, Andrew Rutherford.

The Agreement Act

This Act, known also as the Agreement Act, confirmed the arrangement mentioned. The preamble

The City Creditors' Act, 1838. states that the Agreement had been considered by a Parliamentary Committee who had reported that its terms should be carried into effect, and that the interest payable upon the government debt then amounting to £228,374 ought to be postponed for that purpose, but that no part thereof should be abandoned. It was therefore enacted that the security held by the Treasury over the harbour and docks should be postponed to the annual payment from the Leith revenues of £7680, which sum should be applied as follows :—viz. £2000 for behoof of the city ministers, in consideration of which the duty of a merk per ton was abolished ; £3180 for behoof of the City Creditors, in consideration of which all demands competent to them upon the harbour and docks were discharged ; and £2500 for behoof of the college and schools of the city, in consideration of which all demands competent to the Town Council upon the harbour and docks were similarly discharged. On the other hand it was provided that no claim or demand should thereafter be competent to the Treasury from or against any of the other property or revenues of the Corporation.

The existing statutory provisions with respect to the appointment of a Dock Commission were repealed and a new Dock Commission was set up, in which were vested the harbour and docks and relative properties with ample power for the management thereof. The New Commissioners were eleven in number, of whom five were to be appointed by the Treasury, three by the Town Council of Edinburgh and three by the Town Council of Leith, but, to insure the independence of the new body, it was provided that no Town Councillor should be capable of being elected as a Commissioner.

The City of Edinburgh and the Town of Leith were separated and dissevered in all the civil and municipal relations thereof, and the Common Good and customs of Leith were transferred to the Town Council of Leith with certain properties named. The Town Council of Leith were given an option, which they did not exercise, of purchasing the whole rights of superiority in Leith which belonged to or were vested in the Corporation of Edinburgh ; and another option, which was exercised, to purchase the Links of Leith.

The Town Council of Edinburgh were authorised to compound for their debts by granting to their Creditors bonds of perpetual annuity at the rate of £3 for every £100 of debt, the same to be redeemable by payment of £100 for every £3 of annuity. In security of the annuities certain revenues and properties, specified in a Schedule to the Act, were conveyed to the Creditors and declared to be liable to adjudication in the event of failure to pay the annuities. In another Schedule there was an enumeration of other revenues and properties which were not to form any part of the security to the Creditors except to the extent of £1000 per annum, these being principally the Common Good or customs and market dues. In respect of these properties it was provided that the same should not be alienable by sale or pledge or security, but the revenues thereof should always be applicable to the proper municipal expenses of the city and no other purpose.

In the event of the Creditors proceeding to an adjudication, it was declared that this should be held to be in full discharge of all and every debt and obligation contracted by the Town Council prior to July 1833, and that no accounting to the Town Council would be required. For the purpose of attending to the interests of the Creditors under the Act, a Committee was appointed, their names being John Learmonth, William MacHutcheon, William Macdonald, James Dunsmure and Thomas MacRitchie. The two first named had been appointed Trustees by the Act of 1833.

These were the more important provisions of the Act, which also contained details intended to meet the different contingencies that might arise. The Schedule, which mentions the items of the Common Good inalienably secured to the Corporation, states also the yearly rents at which the customs were then farmed out: thus the customs of the land, cloth, and flesh markets were rented at £1200; the fruit and green markets at £1090, the fish market at £311, the meal and corn market at £456, the House of Muir and Hallow Fair at £410. The schedule of properties conveyed in security to the Creditors covered nearly all the other assets then belonging to the Corporation. Certain of these were, however, declared to be redeemable by the City at prices stated, and were in point of fact so redeemed, as follows:—the Royal Exchange Buildings in 1863 at the price of £3800; the Meadows in 1869 at the price of £7732; the Bruntsfield Links in 1865 at the price of £1896; the Calton Hill in 1867 at the price of £717; the Princes Street Gardens in 1852 at the price of £2685, this last sum coming out of the monies received from the Railway Company when the first lines were laid through the Gardens.

The Sederunt Book of the Committee of the City Creditors may be perused in the City Chambers. According to the first Minute in this book the functions of the Committee were to adjust the claims of the Creditors; to see that the security subjects were not unduly dilapidated; to attend to the regular payment of the annuities; and in the event of any failure, to take steps for adjudging the security subjects and converting the same into money. The Committee appointed as their clerk Mr Alexander Douglas, W.S., who was succeeded by his son, Mr Christopher Douglas, W.S. A joint bank account was kept, and the concurrence of the Committee was asked when any transaction was contemplated which might affect the security subjects. Thus in the year 1857 the Town Council proposed to sell the Portsburgh Court House, and the concurrence of the Committee of Creditors was given on condition that the free proceeds were paid into the joint bank account to be applied at the sight of the Committee in purchasing and cancelling annuity bonds. These bonds, at the passing of the Act, sold on the market at slightly more than £80, so that the Creditors who sold out did so at a sacrifice of 20 per cent. of their capital; but those who held the bonds ultimately received payment in full.

It has been mentioned that the debt due by the city to the Government was extinguished by the

Recent History.

transfer of the docks at Leith from the Corporation to the Dock Commission. The subsequent course of this debt was a matter between the Dock Commission and the Treasury; and in the year 1860 an Act of Parliament was passed providing for the settlement and discharge of this debt. The Act narrated the expenditure of large sums on dock improvements; that the surplus revenues were insufficient to pay off the debt, which stood at the sum of £228,374; that the Dock Commissioners had offered to pay the Treasury a sum of £50,000 in full satisfaction of the said debt and interest thereon; and that the Treasury should be authorised to accept this sum and to grant a discharge to the

The Old City Debt

Dock Commissioners. Accordingly power was given to borrow the amount and the debt was finally extinguished on this basis.

The annual payment of £7680 from the Dock revenues has also been extinguished. Out of this sum £2000 was provided for the city ministers, and in the year 1870 this portion was redeemed by the payment of £40,000 made by the Dock Commission to the Ecclesiastical Commissioners. In 1894, as part of the rearrangement to be mentioned shortly, the Dock Commissioners were authorised to redeem at $33\frac{1}{2}$ years' purchase the remaining portions of the said sum of £7680, that is the payment of £3180 to the City Creditors, and the payment of £2500 for behoof of the college and schools. The sum paid for this redemption in February 1895 was £189,333.

It has been mentioned above that the Creditors did not have the benefit of an assessment or a sinking fund, but both of these advantages were in fact provided by later legislation. Certain of the market customs having been abolished in 1840, a duty was granted in lieu thereof termed the commutation duty. This duty in turn was abolished by the Markets and Customs Act, 1874, which provided for the produce of $\frac{1}{2}$d. per pound of Burgh Assessments being paid to the Common Good as an equivalent for the commutation duty, by way of security to the Creditors of the city on the old city bonds ; and it was further provided that, should the

Edinburgh Stock Act

Creditors proceed to adjudge the security subjects made over by the Agreement Act, such adjudication should extend to and include the annual payment coming in place of the commutation duty. This assessment continued to be paid in aid of the Common Good until 1894.

In that year the assessment ended and the old city debt entered upon a new and final phase by the passing of the Edinburgh Stock Act. This Act gave power to the Corporation to issue stock for all monies borrowed and power to redeem the old city debt annuities at par, which was accordingly done. The Corporation were required to pay annually out of the Common Good revenues towards the redemption of the remaining debt such a sum as would represent one-sixtieth part of the principal, and in this way the balance of the debt was to be paid off by instalments spread over a period of sixty years. Instead of being practically permanent, unless when a payment was made from the proceeds of property realised or from surplus revenues, the debt thus became compulsorily redeemable not later than 1954.

In the year 1895 the debt stood in the books at £295,303. By the application of certain monies, mainly the large amount paid by the Dock Commission as stated above, the debt was summarily redeemed to the round figure of £100,000. The annual contribution towards liquidation was fixed at £1666, 13s. 4d., and year by year this contribution

The Old City Debt

has been entered in the Corporation Accounts so that the process of redemption has been going on by easy stages. The accounts have also shown the payments to the college and the schools, amounting together to the sum of £2500 which has been referred to above. In the year 1925 the remaining debt stood at £49,583, and in 1926 the Corporation Accounts show the ordinary contribution of £1666, 13s. 4d., and they also show a special contribution of £47,916, 13s. 4d., thereby completing the redemption and anticipating the payments which in ordinary course would have gone on for other twenty-eight years. The suggestion to close this chapter in the finances of the city was made by Mr Imrie, in the year of his appointment as City Chamberlain, and when it was given effect to, Mr Imrie had made an end of what might well be called "an auld sang."

CHAPTER X

MERCHANTS AND MARKETS

ALTHOUGH the rise of the Royal Burgh of Edinburgh is lost in the distance of tradition and legend, it may be safe to conclude that it arose because of the protection of the Castle. Whether the first inhabitants were mainly agricultural or not, it is fairly certain that they soon would take up the work of providing the dwellers there with necessary supplies and thus develop into a trading community. A convenient seaport would also help the growth of the town, making it a suitable centre for the trade of the surrounding country with the outside world.

Before the first existing written record, Edinburgh was undoubtedly a place of some size, with mills and the port of Leith, for these and the possession of their burgh were confirmed to the burgesses of Edinburgh in 1329, as held direct from the Crown; and by the Charter of Robert I. it is surely implied that these privileges were no new ones. A Charter of David II. indicates the carrying on of trade within the burgh by the gift of land on which to build a tron. This tron, or place for weighing goods, was an indispensable adjunct to trade, for all merchandise brought to the burgh had to be weighed at one of the two trons, one where the church of that name now stands, the other at the head of the Bow. A Charter of Robert II. in 1386, granting to the burgesses a piece of land in the High Street, used apparently for the building of the first Tolbooth, mentions the market-place of the burgh, while various succeeding Charters show that the trade of Edinburgh must have been of some considerable extent, since Kings could make grants of sums of money from their customs, levied on goods coming into the burgh.

A letter of James I. in 1427 promising to indemnify the four burghs of Edinburgh, Perth, Dundee, and Aberdeen for the sum of 50,000 merks English money, for which they had become caution to the King of England for his ransom, shows that the burghs were tolerably wealthy, and, as in other cases Edinburgh supplied the bulk of such contributions, it is probable that a large part of the required amount came from the Edinburgh merchants.

These, among other documents, are noted as showing how the development of the burgh proceeded by the successive grants of privileges and by Royal interest and protection, and how, with the increase of powers, came increase of prosperity. But to deal with the growth of the trade of Edinburgh would be a lengthy matter, and all that can be attempted is to give some idea of the customs and conditions prevailing among the trading community, who in the sixteenth century formed the bulk of the inhabitants.

Freemen and Unfreemen

Merchandise and trade were carefully regulated, but at what period the various regulations came into force it is not possible to say. The dominant distinction, that between freemen and unfreemen, must have been established long before the *Leges Burgorum* of the reign of David I. took shape, and that was some three hundred years before any existing records of the proceedings of the Magistrates of Edinburgh. Hence, by the beginning of the sixteenth century, the subdivisions of the inhabitants had been long established. The freemen, burgesses, and guild brethren, drawn chiefly from merchants and craftsmen, included also a few to whom the rights were granted as a favour. The unfreemen ranged from gentry, living in the burgh, who did not require to engage in trade and to whom therefore "freedom" with its rights and responsibilities made no appeal, to journeymen and apprentices in course of qualifying for the rank of burgess ; craftsmen whose work was considered too lowly to be organised ; and labourers ; also a floating population of beggars and vagabonds, cripples and sick, representing a grave problem to be faced by the burgh.

It has been said that the old merchant was most nearly related to the general merchant of a small present-day village. If this be limited to the merchant burgess, the comparison is most apt. An act of the Town Council of 1583 states the goods which these might sell : coarse cloths, such as linen, frieze, Yorkshire cloth, kersey, oil, soap, butter, fruit, eggs, figs, raisins, "plowmdames," fish, vinegar : it has the very smell of a country shop! Guild brethren dealt in more dignified and costly wares, wine, wax, woad for dyeing, spices, silks, cloth of gold and silver and fine foreign woollens.

Strict monopolies were the rule in sixteenth-century Edinburgh, probably from a much earlier date. Hence the multiplicity of trades in so comparatively small a town. The crafts were numerous, working under their own seals of cause and supervised by their own deacons. A list of the trades shows how busy a place it must have been. Besides the merchants, a class apart by their privileges and control of the government of the burgh, were the bakers, cooks, skinners, fleshers, furriers, bonnet-makers, masons, wrights, surgeons, apothecaries, goldsmiths and all other smiths, comprised in the guild of the hammermen, weavers, waulkers, shoe-makers, tailors, taverners and innkeepers, each with their work arranged to prevent encroachment and governed by the statutes laid down by the Council which was also designed to ensure stable prices.

These monopolies had their inconveniences, but the Magistrates dealt with each case as it came and did not draw morals which might have been troublesome. At one time the slaters gave much trouble by doing their work slowly and ineffectively. As no one else might do their work, the Council found it difficult to find a punishment when threats were of no avail. The bakers were also apt to be annoying. Statutes were multiplied enjoining them neither to burn nor water their bread, to mark it with the correct weight and their own mark, and to keep the statutory size and price, as laid down from time to time by proclamation. Once they threatened to strike; once it was found necessary to threaten to deprive them of their freedom and find others to take their places if they continued to neglect their work. The furriers once found reason to complain that the tailors were infringing on their rights and taking from them a limited custom by trimming garments with fur. The Council found the grievance justified and took steps to satisfy the furriers, but the incident remains as an illustration of the complication of town life when a merchant sold the material, the tailor made it up, the furrier trimmed it, and the "browdster" or embroiderer added the final touches. The skinners, a few years later, claimed the exclusive right to embroider leather, but the Magistrates decreed that any one who chose had the right to adorn purses and gloves with embroidery to their liking and even to sell it. The fairness of the Town Council is again instanced when they prevented the fleshers from spoiling the market of the "outland" men who brought cattle to sell at the House of the Muir. The fleshers had been in the habit of meeting the herds on the way and of making bargains to their own advantage when the unfree sellers had not the protection of the Town's market regulations and the supervision of the bailies. The Magistrates discussed and condemned the practice and apparently it ceased.

The dignity of freemen of the burgh was maintained by acts of Council, and there were many things which they were not allowed to do. A guild brother could not exercise a craft, so that any who aspired to that rank had to betake himself to the correct sort of merchandise and share the responsibilities of his new position. A burgess must not engage publicly in menial labour: one was censured for removing stones from the High Street in front of his house, at that time undergoing repair. Several times cooks who were made burgesses were warned that they must not carry the dishes prepared by themselves to the purchasers, but must send their servants. Similarly candlemakers made burgesses had to send round candles to their customers with their apprentices.

It would be interesting to know more than the Records tell of some of the old trades. The cooks who are mentioned must have been caterers, useful in supplying the elaborate pies and pastries beyond the capacity or utensils of the ordinary housewife. There were one or two French cooks in Edinburgh, as the accounts of banquets show, and most probably these were not servants but masters of their own establishments. A somewhat similar trade was that of the "sukkerman" or confectioner. Queen Anne, wife of James VI., valued hers so highly that she invited the Council to make him a burgess and guild brother. They seem to have hesitated to do so for they sent a deputation to discuss the matter with the Queen, though the conclusion to which they came is not known. Nothing has been found of the daily avocations of these confectioners, but in times of feasting or public rejoicing they came to their own, for no banquet was complete without their preparations, and at the end of a day of festivity "scrotchertis and confectis," otherwise sweets, used to be scattered among the crowds. Another trade which dealt in luxuries was the apothecary's, barely recognisable as the "ypothecar." By virtue of his trade he was allowed to make and retail spirits or "aquavitæ." He had also the monopoly and probably the secret of another drink, known as "ypocras," used on very festive occasions, of which wine was the foundation, but the rest of the ingredients are left to the imagination of the present day—possibly an early form of cocktail.

It is very evident that in some things the Edinburgh of the past was like the modern town. There must have been little of the self-contained life of the country places, where every one had to be his own baker, brewer, spinner, weaver, cobbler, and other trades. Not all of the town houses had their own ovens, so that baking must have been limited to oatcakes and such food as could be baked on a girdle. These they did possess, one woman being the owner of a five-footed girdle, well-adapted for use on a flat hearth. Many people therefore must have been dependent upon the bakers for their supplies, and apparently hucksters had liberty to sell the coarser kinds of bread and oatcakes. A number of merchants made their own malt, and some must have brewed for themselves, but in 1596 a scheme was set afoot by which the Society of Brewers was formed to supply the town with ale and beer. This dependence on each other was prevented from becoming a means of extorting high prices by the fact that the cost of all articles and the possible profit was regulated by the Council.

The fortunes of traders were subject to considerable fluctuation. Sometimes the wealth and prosperity is marked, and then suddenly a well-to-do merchant might find himself faced with the necessity of asking the help of the Council, either by exemption from taxation or by actual support. Some idea of the possible wealth of the inhabitants of Edinburgh is seen in a list of contributors to a loan to James VI. in 1582. A sum of £4000 had to be found in the town, and it was produced by twenty-one persons, of whom eighteen were merchants, and the rest included one skinner, one goldsmith, Michael Gilbert by name, one taverner, one cook, one maltman, and one other whose occupation was not specified. Of these, Gilbert, the skinner and two merchants contributed 300 li., one of the Napier family gave 400 li., and the rest sums varying from 200 li. to 50 merks. Catering must have been a prosperous

VILLAGE OF DEAN

264

trade enough, for the cook produced 50 li. The other side of the picture is seen in the Records of the Burgh Court to which merchants resorted to obtain payment of debts due to them, perhaps for long periods. One loan dated back for nineteen years. Other transactions in that Court included apprisings and selling-up of stock for debt. Sometimes the end of a merchant's career was such as recorded in an act of Council 1584-5, when, on consideration that John Banks, merchant burgess, had watched, warded and borne all portable charges in the burgh, had been of good repute and had fallen upon evil days, they granted to him the next vacant bedeman's place in the hospital of St Paul's Wark.

The regular trade of the town was carried on in booths or houses. They tended to congregate together, but sometimes mention is made of an isolated shop. The goldsmiths, skinners, and shoe-makers had their shops clustered round St Giles'; others were in the High Street under the galleries of the houses; some shoemakers had booths in the Cowgate, at the foot of the Nether Kirkyard, while in the same street was the first printing-press; a book-binder had his shop near the church; and others, among them the fleshers, worked in the wynds and closes.

There were also itinerant sellers of different goods in the town, though many were barely tolerated by the Magistrates, and statutes were made prescribing the regulations to be enforced against them. Milkmen might cry their milk only at certain hours in the morning—on Sundays only before 7 A.M. Sellers of fruit, flowers, and vegetables were subject to other rules, while the Council discouraged the employment of unmarried women in these capacities.

As regards women, their position in the burgh is interesting enough to be worth comment. While the Council would not allow the employment of unmarried women as hawkers or let them be house-holders, the wives and widows of burgesses held a certain place. Frequently the wife of a merchant kept a shop or a tavern. The widows of merchants and of some craftsmen, notably goldsmiths, seem to have continued to hold their husbands' booths and to carry on business, presumably till the children were old enough to do so. Under such circumstances they were liable to the duties of burgesses, they had to find a substitute for the watch, or, in the event of a levy, for the King's army, and were taxed with others. The Council, however, took their position into consideration and dealt lightly with them on some occasions, and in specially deserving cases interested themselves in the children, arranging apprenticeships for them, either freely or for nominal fees. But at one time, after Flodden, widows were too numerous to have any privileges and bore the full responsibility which would have fallen to their men, providing a man for the watch or finding board and lodging for at least one of the town's armed men. At that time the Council

Market Days

Minutes record neither complaints nor appeals, so that it appears that the women rose to the occasion.

Though there were shops scattered over the town, it was in the markets that the trading life of the burgh would be seen in its most active state, and in the two fairs to which the town was entitled. These were thrown open to inhabitants of the town both free and unfree, and to the people of the adjoining country, the "outland" folk. All were allowed to trade, and unfree persons might put up "crames" or open stalls on certain parts of the High Street for the charge of a $\frac{1}{2}$d. Unfreemen were not allowed to buy till a later hour than freemen, thus maintaining the privileged position of the burgesses, and their goods had to be sold at a slightly higher price. This arrangement, however unfair it may sound, was reasonable enough considering the charges which the burgesses had to bear: the support of the poor of the town, taxes and customs both royal and burghal, the duty of watching and warding, and the liability to extra expenses due to the position of Edinburgh as the capital; whereas the outland men only paid the petty customs at the ports of the town. So heavy were these charges on the burgesses that it was not unknown for them to renounce their position, preferring the calculable inconveniences of being unfree.

Markets in early days seem to have been frequent. A Statute of 1478 gives the days for the sale of provisions as Mondays, Wednesdays, and Fridays. In 1526 the Magistrates ordered that bread should be sold on those days, while flesh was to be sold in the markets on Sundays, Mondays, and Thursdays. Thus five days of the week at least brought people to the town. The Reformation put an end to the Sunday market, and the General Assembly in 1592 desired the Council to change the Monday market to Wednesday, on the ground that people coming from the country to attend the market were apt to start on the Sabbath. The change was effected, not without criticism, for some held that it was none of the Council's business when these people started, but as to "thaim that came far off, it became the pastors of thair parochins to hinder thaim." The Statute shows from what distances men came to buy and sell in Edinburgh, seeing that the Council sent letters intimating the change to towns so far off as Glasgow, Ayr, Selkirk, and Jedburgh.

The earliest known situation of the markets is given in a letter of James III. under his privy seal, dated 1477. They changed in later years, but the list serves to show how crowded the town must have been on such days. The hay, straw, grass. and horse-food market was in the Cowgate from Forrester's Wynd to Peebles' Wynd, fish in the same street from Blackfriars' Wynd to the Netherbow, salt in Niddry's Wynd, the stalls of the chapmen on the north side of the High Street from the Bellhouse or Tolbooth to the Tron, the hatmakers and skinners

The First Covered Market

facing them on the south side, wood from Dalrymple's yard to Greyfriars, shoemakers from Forrester's Wynd to the dyke of that yard and tanned leather in the same place, wild-fowl and other poultry round the Market Cross, meat round the Tron and as far as Blackfriars' Wynd, cattle outside the West Port near the King's Stables, meal in the High Street from the Tolbooth to Liberton's Wynd, cloth above that, butter and cheese and wool at the Over Bow, iron-work of all sorts beneath the Netherbow, and old clothes beside Greyfriars.

To go into all the changes of position would be long and serve no useful purpose, since the latest position of the more important markets are fixed in the names known to most people of to-day. One less known change is worth recording. The Town Council seem to have considered at different times the desirability of having a covered place where they could sell and buy in comfort—what wonder, if the climate of the past was like that of the present! Possibly the merchants who traded with France and Flanders were the authors of the suggestion. A proposal was made in 1552 and came to nothing, but in 1601 the Council undertook the construction of a covered market at the foot of the Nether Kirkyard. It was made of wood and proved a source of considerable expense to the Town Treasurer, who found it needful to borrow money in his own name to finance the undertaking. It was known as the Mealmarket or Halls. The effort seems to have exhausted the Council, who made no effort to provide further shelter for other markets.

The concourse of people to the town on market days was the source of much work to the Magistrates. A part of the Bailies' duties was the supervision of the markets, while the Council multiplied statutes as to hours and prices. Much of this care was caused by the offences of the persons known as "forestallers and regraters," those who bought before the markets were thrown open or before wares had been presented to the town and the prices fixed, and those who bought in the markets to retail again at higher prices. These, particularly the regraters, when caught were subject to penalties which seem severe, being sometimes punished with confiscation of their goods and banishment. The Council's intention, however, is clear : the markets were intended for people buying supplies for their households, and buying at the regulation price to sell again at a profit meant something like profiteering in the necessities of life.

The right of having stalls on the High Street was confined to market days, when both free and unfree might have their movable wooden stalls or " crames," covered or uncovered, on certain conditions. The unfree stall-holders, chapmen, or " stallangers " were allowed to rent their stalls for a year at two shillings, for use in time of markets and free fairs. An act of Council of 1481 explains the conclusion to which the Council came as regards this right. The poor stallangers, who could not afford the expense of becoming burgesses, were allowed to rent their places for each year, while those who could become burgesses if they chose were allowed their stalls for one year only and then had to become burgesses or leave the town.

There was much to do for the town officials in the markets. There were the rents of stalls to collect, and these were evaded whenever possible. There were people who purchased the right to hire out boards on which to stand the flour sacks or the fish, the meat or butter, and they had to be watched to see that they asked the correct price. Others used weights and measures not of the statutory kinds, and others tried to evade having their goods weighed at the town trons. There were "flesher wives" who quarrelled, scolded, and swore in the open market, and people who squabbled over the quality of the goods and insisted on being allowed to choose the largest fish for their money, instead of taking them as they came. There were brawlers and riotous apprentices, out for a little amusement on any pretext, good or bad, and other disturbers of the town's peace. With all these the Bailies and their officers dealt faithfully, either by rough justice on those caught red-hand, or by arrest and confinement in that far from salubrious spot the Tolbooth, to await the cooler judgment of the Council on the following day. No wonder that the Bailies considered themselves hard-worked officials, as they did not neglect to show when they thought it advisable.

It was worth the Council's while to attract strangers to the burgh markets, for a considerable part of the Common Good was derived from the petty customs taken at the ports of the town from all goods entering there. The practice was to set the different parts of the Common Good to the highest bidders, leaving to them the trouble of the collection. The value of these tacks is a useful index to the prosperity of the town and to its growth, even allowing for a certain depreciation of the coinage. In rather more than a hundred years they varied as follows: in 1481 the petty customs were set for 116 merks; in 1553 for 480 merks; in 1557, a disturbed year, for 280 pounds; in 1560, another bad year, for 300 merks; in 1565 for 450 merks; in 1581 for 873 li.; in 1583 for 1410 merks, in 1593 for 970 li.; and in 1603 for 1300 merks.

Little is said about the fairs on All Hallow Even and Trinity Even. A letter of James IV. in 1507 determined the date on which the fairs were to be held, for avoidance of the profanation of holy days. The All Hallow Fair was altered to the 4th of November and the eight days following, and Trinity Fair to the Monday following Trinity Sunday. The All Hallow Fair still is held, for a week from the second Monday in November, and is still opened by the Lord Provost and Magistrates. Trinity Fair is no more, but the weekly cattle

STOCKBRIDGE FROM ST BERNARD'S

market at the House of the Muir, held till 1560 on Sundays and thereafter changed to Thursday, might now almost be said to hold its place, for on the two first Mondays in April the House of Muir and Edinburgh store sheep market is held. It is unfortunate that, as in so many other matters, the Council were too accustomed to their fairs to feel the need of recording anything but changes and difficulties.

A feature of the day of the All Hallow Fair was the ceremony of riding the Burgh's marches. The neighbours were summoned by proclamation and appeared ready mounted at the house of the Provost, and accompanied him, the Magistrates and Council, round all the boundaries of the burgh. It was not an optional appearance, and the penalty for absence was 10 li., a sufficiently substantial sum to make attendance desirable. The date of the riding of the marches was at one time changed to Trinity Even, but was again altered to the old date. Apart from that and from occasional references to pipers and drummers on the Fair Day and to the enforcement of regulations about customs and dues, there is no account of the proceedings or of the principal goods sold. One of these dues was the perquisite of the Provost. It was the practice to exact a fee at the ports for the purchase of an ox for him. This fee, known either as the "Provost's ox" or as the "Sheriff's gloves," in allusion to his office as Sheriff of Edinburgh, was not always sufficient for the purchase, a matter of annoyance to the Council when they had to make up the price. Although it is mentioned chiefly as regards the Provost, an entry of 1578 makes it appear that the dues outside the ports belonged to him, and those collected inside to the Bailies, as Sheriffs-Depute. It seems possible that the town officers shared in the perquisites of the Sheriff's gloves, as in 1557 a half pipe of wine was given to them in compensation for the loss of dues, forbidden at the fair of that year. But these are isolated instances, and the bulk of the allusions mention the Provost alone.

The customs collected on these occasions were 4d. a head for cattle and 4d. for every ten sheep entering the West Port. In 1580 the collector of these dues took 6 li. 8s. 4d., a sum too small to defray the cost of the Provost's ox, the price of which had to be made up from the Common Good. In the following year 8 li. was collected, but the ox cost 16 li. 6s. 8d. In 1582 the amount collected was 10 merks, but the price of oxen was still higher, for the Treasurer had to pay out 18 merks more. It would appear that the Town Council had been used to larger receipts; still at these times a considerable number of cattle and sheep must have passed the port. For if half the dues were derived from cattle and half from sheep, in 1581 there must have been 240 of the former and 2400 of the latter, enough surely to indicate some considerable trade.

CHAPTER XI

THE WILD ADVENTURES

THE title sounds exaggerated for the douce and quiet narrative of Edinburgh trade, but it is the one used by the Town Council from the beginning. There was more danger than meets the eye in the voyages made by merchants of the "guid toun" to the ports frequented by them in the Baltic, in Flanders, on the Channel and in the Bay of Biscay, and the Wild Adventures did not wholly belie their name. In modern days it is hard to realise what risks attended the small sailing ships as regards navigation, imperfect knowledge of rocks and shoals, contrary winds, which could cause delay for weeks, storms and hostile ships.

The idea of trade and voyages was an early one in Scotland though the beginnings are not recorded. The Burgh Laws of David II. admitted the absence of a burgess abroad as being sufficient excuse for non-compearance in a case. The Court of the Four Burghs dealt with rules for merchandise brought to Scotland. The chronicler Fordun commented on the foreign trade during the reign of Alexander III. The probability is that the earliest trade was in the hands of foreign merchants, and the early guild laws show that it was carried on without much encouragement from the authorities.

As with all early trade, the Wild Adventures started as a monopoly of the brethren of the guild in Edinburgh and elsewhere. Acts of Parliament and of the Convention of Burghs made clear that such trade should have been the exclusive right of freemen, but regulations concerning the dues payable by unfreemen prove that the monopoly was not easy to enforce. It would have been difficult to exact that the skippers and crews of the ships that brought the goods should be debarred from all share in the ventures, but when merchandise arrived in Scotland the monopoly was enforced. None but merchants might have the retailing of the goods; all unfreemen owning imported goods had to sell to merchant burgesses and pay the special customs levied upon all " unfree traffiquers," so that in spite of relaxation of the regulations, the foreign trade remained a virtual monopoly of privileged persons.

The trade of the whole country, though a comparatively small matter, cannot be dealt with in a paper which only concerns Edinburgh. There were other ports, notably those on the east coast, which carried on their ventures with the same foreign ports. The Scottish History Society, in Volume 28 of the first series, gives the shipping lists of Dundee, in so far as they exist, between the years 1580 and 1618, showing the number of ships returning from abroad with imports. The figures

Foreign Trade

show that the town had a fair overseas trade: in 1581, thirty-eight ships returned with cargoes; in 1582, seventeen; in 1588, sixty-nine. These were from France, Flanders, Norway and the Baltic. The entries give the names of the owners and of the ships, and details as to the cargoes. The *Compt Buik of Alexander Wedderburne*, which forms the first part of that volume, supplies other details. Another source of information as to the Wild Adventures is the *Ledger of Andrew Haliburton*, with which is printed the *Book of Customs and Valuation of Merchandice in Scotland*. The former shows the amount of fifteenth-century trade with Flanders of one merchant, the latter how imports in the early years of the seventeenth century outnumbered exports, and provided not only the luxuries but the necessities of life for a country whose manufactures were very limited.

In the Edinburgh records the early allusions to trade are scanty and deal indirectly with the subject, being concerned chiefly with questions of customs and harbour dues. One entry in 1437-8 may be taken as noting an old trading connection with Bruges. "It is statute that quhat persouns frauchtis a schip owtwart sall gif a sek fraucht to Sanct Rynanes Ile in Brugis, and quhat persouns frauchtis ane schip hamewart thai sall pay a tun fraucht to Sanct Geillis wark."

Royal charters tend to confirm the importance of the town as a centre of trade. The Charter of Robert I.

The Wild Adventures

in 1329 confirms to the burgesses "*predictum Burgum de Edinburgh una cum portu de Leth*": a Charter of James I., in 1428, authorises the taking of certain tolls from all boats entering the harbour of Leith: other similar ones were granted by James II. in 1445 and 1454: James III. granted in 1471, and again in 1482, certain customs to be collected for the repair of the port of Leith: a Charter of James IV. granted the port of Newhaven to the burgh.

The earliest references to trade with France and Flanders in the records seem to be in 1513 and 1514, but the worthy Council cannot be called systematic in their chronicles of the stages of the Wild Adventures. It may be that in times of national or town troubles the trade diminished to a negligible quantity, or that at such times they had too much on their minds to pay attention to lesser matters. But any period of lax administration of the affairs of the merchants was followed by another in which the Council made amends for their slackness by increasing their supervision of the foreign trade.

The entry of ships at the port of Leith was one of the duties of the Dean of Guild, and their numbers and the payments received are rendered in his accounts. The presence of French troops during the regency of Mary of Lorraine seems to have made little difference to Scottish trade, save that there is no return for the year 1558-9. This may be due to the fact that a great part of the town's trade was with

Shipping

France, though Flanders, Dantzig, Stralsund, Veere and other towns, figure in the information given in the Council register, as will be seen later. The list is not so detailed as the Dundee shipping lists and does not discriminate between incoming and outgoing boats, but a table has been drawn up from the entries of successive years to show the comparative numbers. The fee charged for the entry of a ship was 14s.

Year.	Number of Ships.	Dues Received.
1552-3 . . .	76	53 li. 4s.
1553-4 . . .	92	64 li. 8s.
1554-5 . . .	85	59 li. 10s.
1555-6 . . .	76	53 li. 4s.
1556-7 . . .	66	46 li. 4s.
1557-8 . . .	76	53 li. 4s.
1560 . . .	55	38 li. 10s.
1560-1 . . .	99	69 li. 8s.
1561-2 . . .	88	61 li. 12s.
1562-3 . . .	80	56 li.
1563-4 . . .	85	59 li. 10s.
1564-5 . . .	69	48 li. 6s.
1565-6 . . .	78	54 li. 12s.
1566-7 . . .	96	60 li. 4s.

Sixty-six of these ships are also mentioned in the Council Records : six between 1552 and 1556, and the rest in the following two years, for various reasons ranging from unlawful lading to the registration of passengers in outgoing vessels. In most cases the names of the skippers and owners are given, among which are none of the old seafaring families of Leith. Three French traders are mentioned, two of them skippers of an outward-bound boat laden with coal,

John Mat and Ewin Mesolat, Bretons, and Guillaume Tilyear, who brought a cargo of wine and attempted to leave the port without paying duty on four lasts of salmon. Of the total number of ships fifty-five are noted as outward bound. The destination is not always exactly given, the general description being usually France or Flanders, though Normandy and Picardy are named, as also Dieppe, Campvere, Dantzig and "Quenisburg." The cargoes are not specified in all cases, but such exports as hides, salt and salmon are named. Curiously enough there is no question of wool, the most important Scots export. Many of the ships were booked as carrying merchants abroad, in one case as many as thirteen on one ship. These came from various towns in the Lowlands, but for the most part from the "good town" itself, men with well-known Edinburgh names. Some of the names of the boats are worth quoting : the *Mary Fortune*, the *Mary Grace*, the *Hart*, the *Post of the Ferry*, the *Marlyeon*, the *Lawrence*, the *Huguenot*, the *Flying Angel*, the *Trinity*, the *Howlett*, the *Yellow Bark*, the *Black Meg*, the *Hare*, the *Swan*, the *Little Lyon* and the *Golden Bells*.

In 1554-5 the three skippers of the *James*, the *Andrew*, and the *Trinity* offered their services to the Council in peace and war. The offer sounds perfectly straightforward, but the magistrates must have known their men, for they accused them of wanting an excuse to sail to unfree ports and declined

Trinity College Church and Hospital

The Wine Trade

their services. An act of 1555 marks the continual struggle with unfreemen about foreign trade, but seems to wink at it when it enjoined that all ships lading from France or Flanders were to give preference to freemen's goods. It seems probable that the town endeavoured to compensate itself for the loss of the exclusive right by the extra revenue obtained from the unfree traders, who were usually the skippers and crews of the ships.

The wine trade provided a large part of the Edinburgh imports, and in consequence a tolerably detailed account of it is found in the records of the Council. Most of the burgesses must have held large stocks, as can be seen by such references as that to a certain man who could produce nine tuns of wine for a special gift to the King. Apart from private cellars, there were many taverns in Edinburgh, where people, who would not do so in modern days, were not ashamed to keep taverns, managed by their wives or servants. The wife of a Common Clerk of Leith sold wine; several writers in Edinburgh had taverns, and it seems to have been considered a cherished privilege rather than a career of doubtful respectability. The season of the arrival of the wine fleet in late autumn or early winter was a busy one for the Council. The prices of the wine had to be fixed, if possible before the cargoes were unloaded, otherwise the wine had to be stored in cellars in Leith till permission was given for the sale. The responsibility of pricing prior to 1587

had lain with the Provost, Bailies and Council of
the burgh, with the sole condition that the King, his
nobles and gentlemen had to be served first. Some
suspicion seems to have arisen that the importers
might be members of Council and have too great
a say in the matter, so an Act of Parliament of
James VI. in 1587 prescribed a new arrangement
for pricing of wine and timber. There were to be
two representatives of the shire, barons or landed
men; two representatives nominated by the King
and his Council, living either in the burgh or within
six miles of it; and four chosen by the Town Council.
If the representatives of the shire and of the King
should not appear upon forty-eight hours' notice,
the burgh representatives were free to set the prices.
This left matters on the whole much as they were,
for, as the Council records show, the former did
not often think fit to put in an appearance and the
work fell to the men of the burgh. The method of
setting the prices followed the same course each year.
The merchant importers stated on oath the price
paid in France, or showed a certificate from the
port of lading and declared the freight paid. The
Council settled the rate of exchange and the allowance for leakage, added that and the carriage to the
price, made allowance for profits and fixed the price
in Scots money. Having done so, they issued a
proclamation giving the cost per pint. One condition
which sounds strange to modern ears, was that new
wine should cost more than old.

Cost of Wines

The following table of prices may serve to show the approximate cost for a period of fifty years.

Year.	Wines.	French Price.	Scots Price.	Price per Pint.
1556	Bordeaux	...	24 li.	12d.
	Sherry	...	20 li.	10d.
1561	Malvoisie	...	27 li.	...
1564	Bordeaux	...	25 and 30 li.	14d.
	Sherry	...	35 li.	...
1566	Bordeaux	...	36 li.	14d.
1567	"	31 *livres*	36 li.	16d.
	Small wines	25 *livres*	36 li.	16d.
1569	Bordeaux	...	38 li.	16 and 20d.
	Rochelle	...	...	16d.
1570	Bordeaux	...	50 li.	20d.
	Rochelle	...	...	16d.
1571	*Amyeacter*	...	40 li.	...
1575	Bordeaux	...	150 li.	5s. 4d.
	Rough wines	...	...	8, 10, and 12d.
1580	Bordeaux	25 crowns	76 li.	...
	Claret	24 "	...	...
	Hautepays	18 "	61 li.	...
	Rochelle	23 "	78 li.	...
1582	...	19 "	76 li.	3s.
1583	Bordeaux	17, 18, and 19 crowns	76 li.	3s.
	White wine	13 crowns	60 li.	2s. 8d.
1584	Bordeaux	19 "	74 li.	...
1585	"	18 "	74 li.	3s.
1586	Spanish	...	102 li. 10s., a pipe	...
	Bordeaux	40 crowns	146 li.	5s. 8d.
1587	"	...	151 li.	...
1589	"	...	...	6s. 4d.
1596	...	...	190 li.	...
	Bordeaux	...	200 li.	8s.
1599	"	...	229 li. 10s.	...
	Vin sec	...	101 li. 6s. 8d.	...
1601	...	...	240 li.	...
1605	...	...	146 li.	...
1606	...	...	156 li.	...
1607	...	...	220 li.	...

During that time the exchange fluctuated between 16s. and 22s. scots to the *livre* or *franc*.

The steady rise in the cost of wine is interesting,

being very marked in the fifty years shown, partly because it gives some idea of the wealth of a town which could deal extensively in so costly a commodity. With regard to the price of the pint, it must be remembered that the Scots pint represented three modern pints.

Most of the wines were from French ports, with an occasional cargo from Spain. The chief ports were Bordeaux and Rochelle. There were different varieties of wine imported, but it is hardly the work of an amateur to discriminate between the different kinds or to translate them into modern terms. They are named as follows: Bordeaux, of which there were two kinds, Town and Hautepays, Rochelle, sherand or sherry, claret, *vin sec* or sek, Amyeacter, rough wine and small wine. Some of these may be synonymous, but they all are used on different occasions to describe the cargoes.

The tack of the King's customs held by the burghs was paid partly in wines for His Majesty's use. The amount to be provided rose from twenty-six to thirty tuns in 1583, and was subject to increase on particular occasions. An Act of Council in January of that year directed a Bailie to accompany Jerome Bowie, the King's "sumlyer," to Leith to see him provided with the best and readiest wines for the Royal use, the price of which the Provost and Council bound themselves to repay to the merchants from whom it was taken before midsummer.

It is not possible to discuss the trade interests of

The Scottish Staple

Edinburgh without considering to some extent the affairs common to the Royal Burghs, for the good town in this, as in other matters, frequently was called upon to act for them. Edinburgh, being both the capital and the wealthiest town in Scotland, had a preponderating interest and most available money for current expenses.

The affairs of the Scottish Staple in the Netherlands have been dealt with by various writers, and the only thing worth noting is how much of the business of the Staple fell to be managed by the magistrates of Edinburgh. There are allusions to business transacted with the Conservator about the Staple port. How much was left to them is shown by an entry of 1578, remarkable as it illustrates the powers possessed by a committee of the Town Council for settling a matter which concerned all the burghs. On this occasion the powers which they could delegate seem to have required no approval of any other interested parties.

"The quhilk day Alexander Uddert, and Henry Charteris, bailies, Louk Wilsoun, dene of gild, Johnne Arnot, Mr Johnne Prestoun, William Naper, Henry Nesbet, William Lytill, Johnne Adamsoun, Alexander Guthre, James Guthre, Mr Mychael Chisholme, Robert Kar, elder, and Thomas Myller of the counsale efter ressouning upoun the caussis of the staple, seing the samyn can nocht be suddanelie placit nor concludit in respect of the danger of the tyme, and understanding Maister

George Hacket thair conservitur is rady to depairt
to Flanderis, It is thocht guid that the said conservitur interand in commoning with the townes of
Antwearp, Bruges, Campheer, Berrie, Middilburgh
or ony other towne in the Law Cuntreis meit for
the stapill, conform to sic instructiones as salbe
interchangeablie subscryvet be the said conservitur
and the secretar and commoun clerk of this burgh,
giveing powar only to the said conservitur to
commoun in generall termes with the magistrates
of the saidis townes tuiching the planting of the
said stapill, nocht to conclude but the ansuer of
everie towne quha will offer maist for the said stapill
wryttin agane be him with dilligens conform to the
instructiones following."

The instructions follow in great detail, but do
not differ greatly from those printed elsewhere. The
consideration of the number of the Scottish demands
is productive of wonder that the Flemish towns ever
found it worth while to compete for the privilege
of receiving the small amount of the trade of
Scotland.

Lesser matters of discipline with regard to the
Conservator were settled offhand by the Town
Council. In 1573 they declared that Hacket must,
as his predecessors had done, pay duty on the
goods which he imported. In 1576-7 they seem to
have meddled with his private possessions, for the
Treasurer was ordered to give to the customer 8 li.
for the customs of Mr George Hacket, which they

The Conservator's Duties

forbade him to receive because he had been summoned
to come to Scotland on the common affairs. They
interposed in 1579 to forbid unlawful exactions by
him in levying a tax on goods landed in Flanders
for his own benefit, on this occasion however acting
as the mouthpiece of the Convention of Burghs.
In 1581 a letter was sent to Hacket dealing with a
complaint by certain merchants that he detained their
goods in the Staple at Veere, compelling them to
sell there instead of seeking better markets inland,
as they were entitled to do. Again in the same
year, the Council appointed a committee to discuss
with the Conservator the matters to be laid before
the next Convention of Burghs. Although the
records seem to deal largely with the difficulties
of the working of the Staple, occasionally an entry
throws light on the uses of the office, as in 1583-4
when a letter of the Council required him to see
to the affairs of one of the Scots factors at Veere,
who had died in debt to certain merchants. But
it cannot have been an easy job to maintain the
position of Conservator in Flanders, to reconcile
the demands of the Burghs with the policy of the
magistrates of Veere, and particularly to serve his
masters in Scotland from so great a distance, with
the knowledge that he might be called upon at
short notice to make the stormy journey to Leith
to answer for his actions to the Town Council of
Edinburgh as well as to the whole Convention.

Little indication is given of the nature of the

exports and imports in the records, except as
regards attempts to prevent forbidden trade in food.
In spite of regulations to the contrary, merchants
constantly seem to have tried to send grain abroad,
and the Council exercised a wide jurisdiction as
regards prevention, concerning themselves not only
with shipping at Leith but with the doings of the
coast towns of Fife. In 1583 an act of Council
commanded two bailies to go to Leith to seize the
cargo of wheat and flour which they had learned that
a man of Dysart was about to export. They were
successful in their errand, and the twelve barrels of
"mayne" or fine flour intended for sale abroad were
confiscated to the town's use. What was done with
the flour does not transpire, but it was surely too
valuable to be given, as happened with any damaged
goods, to the hospital or the lepers. The imports
noted included wine, fruit, and vegetables, among
which apples, oranges, "ungyeons," peas and beans
are specially noted, spices and salt. Most of the
stock-in-trade of burgesses and guild brethren came
from abroad, fine woollens from England, and all
luxuries in the way of dress from France, Flanders
and Italy, Scottish manufactures not having reached
a point of skill beyond the weaving of coarse woollen
and linen cloth. The very names of materials and
garments prove that both fashions and stuffs came
from abroad, introduced by merchants or in the
wardrobes of Scots gentlemen and soldiers of fortune.
The names and descriptions occurring in different

records of the Burgh show that the Scotsman, like Portia's English suitor, picked up his clothes anywhere and everywhere. Mention is found of a suit of "fulyie morte" satin, hose of "incarnat" silk, breeches made "after the Myllane fassoun," breeches of "Londoun claithe," a mantle of the "Gascun fassoun," and "Romany vyolettis," the last-named being apparently a kind of purple satin from Rome.

In days when freedom of trade even between town and town was undreamt of, it is easy to see what restrictions must have hedged about all export and import of commodities. This matter, which concerned all the burghs, fell, like other pieces of business, to Edinburgh for regulation. The question of the customs in France was left frequently to the magistrates, who seem to have taken the responsibility for granted. In 1564 mention is made of their letters to the factors at Dieppe, recommending Edinburgh merchants to them, though the service desired was not stated. In 1568 the Council was engaged in negotiations about the French customs, for they required a translation of a permission obtained for them previously by a certain Captain Cockburne, who had served in the French King's Scots Guard. This permission concerned a reduction of 16d. in the franc in the Rouen customs. In 1579-80, Henry Nesbett, bailie, with such as he might choose, was ordered to go to the Privy Council to petition for the removal of some new customs. In the same year there is an amusing glimpse given of town dissensions. A well-known burgess, Adam Fullerton, who had fallen into disfavour with the merchants of the town over the business he had transacted in England, announced that common rumour accused him of being the cause of the increased customs, and asked that the slander might be tried by the magistrates. So far as can be seen, it was probably a case of a bad name. Fullerton, deputed some years previously to attempt to obtain compensation for the depredations of English pirates, had been accused of intending to decamp to the Low Countries with the money. Though the truth of the allegation had not been definitely proved, he was, as a consequence, unpopular in the town. This slander of which he complained, by which he was accused of having caused the increased customs on all exports, was apparently another manifestation of the prejudice against him. The Council seem to have regarded it as such, for they acknowledged his grievance by allowing him the inquiry desired. But, as too frequently occurred, the result was not recorded. In 1581 considerable trouble seems to have arisen over a new scale of French customs. The King was approached on the matter of the new dues on Scots cloth, a letter was sent to the factors at Dieppe, but the records do not give the text of the letter with the grounds of complaint. The question dragged on into the next year, when the Council applied to the King and the Privy Council for their assistance

The Farming of the Customs

in obtaining a reduction. Finally the step was taken of sending Henry Nesbett, an influential merchant, to the King of France. He was furnished with credentials from James VI. and the Council guaranteed to him the sum of 2000 francs for his expenses, stipulating the rate of exchange, then 18s. to the franc. There again, so far as the acts of Council go, was an end of the affair, except as regards future reference to paying their envoy's expenses.

The Council followed the general practice of farming out the customs of the Wild Adventures to the highest bidder each year, as they did other parts of the Common Good. It happened occasionally that they thought well to keep them in their own hands, and, though not expressly stated, it seems that the step was taken because the magistrates found ground to suspect that the farmers of the customs were making too much profit from their bargain.

Considerable difficulty was always experienced in collecting the customs dues. There were two standards, one for freemen and the other for unfreemen, and though the town winked at the import of goods by the latter, they were careful to exact the larger dues from them and any suspected of using them for purposes of trading. One man who had forfeited his freedom by living in Leith was obliged to pay unfreemen's customs for all his goods, including the cargo of the *Graip* of Crail. Timothy

The Wild Adventures

Cagnioli, Italian, burgess of Edinburgh, having become caution for the goods of Symon Lastrik, "Dutcheman," was compelled to pay both free and unfree customs. Another merchant, William Cunninghame, caution for the *Jonas* and the *Grewhound* of Anstruther, laden with French wheat and barley, had to pay unfree customs for the part of the cargo owned by the skippers, who were not freemen.

In addition to the petty customs of the town, there had to be considered the King's customs on exports and imports. This vexed question, though dealt with by the Convention of Burghs, was also referred to the Council. In 1582 the Treasurer paid the expenses of a deputation sent to the King at Perth to complain of innovations introduced by the Lords of Exchequer. Later the Council considered the terms of the contract between the King, the Privy Council, and the Controller on the one part, and the Burghs on the other, concerning the tack of these customs, particularly the part in which the dues payable by Edinburgh, Perth, Dundee, and Aberdeen were specified, after which they allowed their commissioners to sign. It was probably a profitable arrangement all round, for the King promptly borrowed on the strength of it the sum of 1000 li., equally promptly borrowed for the purpose by the lenders, the "Good Town." The heavy burdens laid on trade are shown in an entry which concerned a tax levied to pay the expenses of a commissioner to France. This was levied upon exports in addition to the usual customs. The extra charge amounted to 6 li. on every hundred lamb-skins, 12 li. on leather, and a lesser sum on re-exports, 2s. on the tun of wine, 4s. on the ship pound of wax, 2s. on the "last" of pitch, tar, and soap. When the dues for import and re-export were added, the wonder is that the struggling Scots trade could bear such burdens even for a short time, and not suffer too greatly to make recovery impossible.

That the Wild Adventures occasionally justified their name may be seen from the Council records. Troubles came upon the merchants from enemies, pirates, and storms. In the latter part of the sixteenth century, when a state of comparative peace prevailed, the greatest dangers were from pirates and rough weather. English and other ships seem to have found Scots merchants a tempting prey. The sufferers complained to anyone convenient, Regent, King, Privy Council, or Town Council. The last-named encouraged them to take matters into their own hands, even helping them with the equipment of ships. In justice it must be said that the Scots on occasion could be guilty too and even their allies of France. In 1558 there is a note of payment made to town officers for guarding three Frenchmen in the Tolbooth, accused of attempting to take a ship from the roads of Leith. In 1561 a reward was given to another officer who captured at Kirkcaldy a ship which had left the harbour of Leith suspected of piracy. In 1567 a certain John Edmistoun, imprisoned in the Tolbooth for piracy, was executed. The Act of Council which recorded this treated it as an aside, the important question being an unlawful claim by the jailor to bedding provided for the prisoner by a woman of the town. In 1580 the Provost wrote to the King about John Cockburne, lately turned pirate, and a year later mention was made of a ship arriving at Burntisland with merchandise plundered from the English. Whether such reprisals met with genuine disapproval is doubtful, but on one occasion at least the Council assisted an Englishman, John Doull of Bristol, plundered in Loch Broom, to obtain compensation. He must have had much influence somewhere, for the Council, consulted as to what was to be done, reported " We haif concludit it salbe mair esie for our nichtbouris quhilkis war allegeit troublaris of Dowle, Inglisman, to give for cutting away of farther troublis and intertaining of amitie alevin scoir ten pundis sterling money (£230) . . . albeit as we ar surelie informit his schip and haill guidis was nocht worth the soume abonewrittin be far."

Still the Scots undoubtedly suffered much from the English, and frequent complaints were recorded. In 1575 merchants returning from Flanders were plundered by pirates, and the Convention of Burghs decreed that each was to bear an equal share of the loss. In 1577 matters had come to such a pass that the Town Council despatched one of the neighbours, Adam Fullerton, to England with complaints to the Queen and Council. He was provided with letters from the Regent Morton, and 900 merks for his expenses. During his absence the town apparently refrained from reprisals, for a certain Patrick Cranstoun complained that he had been appointed captain against the pirates, had missed a voyage on that account, had collected soldiers, only to find the expedition abandoned. The Council admitted some justice in his complaint and paid him 100 merks compensation. Meanwhile Fullerton had some measure of success in his embassy, for he sent a commission under the Great Seal from the Lord High Admiral of England for examining witnesses to the charges of piracy. He was absent for many months in England and contrived to incur the suspicion of his fellow-burgesses, who informed the King that he had been successful in recovering large sums of money, but intended to decamp to Flanders, there to live in peace with his family on the money belonging to his neighbours. So the unfortunate envoy was imprisoned in the Tolbooth till he should find caution to hand over the vast sums he was supposed to hold. There is a hint that Fullerton was not so successful as was imagined in the great difficulty he was at to recover even a part of his expenses. In 1585 the pirates of England again proved troublesome, and Henry

The Wild Adventures

Nesbett with some others was sent to the King to obtain permission to fit out ships against them. James promised to grant the permission if the representations of the English ambassador to his mistress did no good. Private adventures were not unknown, such as one in 1590, when William Sibbet borrowed 200 li. on the security of his own lands in order to pursue English pirates. In 1610, pirates who made Orkney their base and were a terror to Scots trade, were pursued by three skippers of Leith, financed by the Town Council. The venture was successful, their ship was captured and the spoils amounted to 13,094 li. 15s. 3d. This money was divided between the parties concerned in the capture, proportionately to their risk, after all expenses had been paid, the captain receiving 650 merks.

Other adventures narrated or hinted at were due to storms. The story of the ship almost wrecked on the Goodwin Sands is given in the Burgh Charters in the form of a deed of gift to Trinity College in 1587 by a company of Scots merchants. The "zelous and godlie personis" who made the donation of 1000 merks to the hospital to be invested for its purposes, being in danger of their lives, and narrowly escaping shipwreck "far by manis expectatioun" collected the sum in contributions according to their means, and the names of the givers and their gift are on record to this day. A similar story is that of John Robertson

and his "complices," who "for performing of thair
vow maid upoun sey being in extreme danger of
thair lyffes," planned and built a new leperhouse at
the Rood of the Greenside.

One interesting part of the regulations for
foreign trade is the "scatt," a contribution made
to equalise the losses arising from sacrifices made
for the common safety during storms, or from
plundering by pirates. The Convention of Burghs
legislated for such cases in 1575-6: "In cais ony
schippis be pilleit, the gudis saiff sall contribute
scatt and loitt for the releif of the personis dampny-
feit, bayth schip and gudis according to thair
wairing : . . . and the samyn ordour to be keipit
anent the gudis casten for saiftie of lyfe and gudes
upoun commoun consent." This was confirmed by
the Convention in July 1580, with the further
stipulation that "no cloithis nor other geir quhat-
sumevir within sey kistis cassin or pilleit sall scatt
and lot with the uther gudis and merchandreis
cassin or pilleit, as alsua na uther gudis imput in
the schip at na uther port nor at hir ladning port,
salbe haldin to scat and lot." The arrangement
secured that no loss should be borne by a few, but
was divided proportionately between all the
merchants, the owner, skipper, and crew of the
ship. The business of setting the scatt seems to
have been usually one of difficulty, subject as it
was to much discussion and many inquiries, some
of which had to be in foreign parts. The task of

assembling the injured parties to give evidence, and of giving judgment as to the proportion of damages was unpopular with the Council, judging by the reluctance with which it was carried through.

Two cases of scatt are on record in the Council Register, and, as they serve to throw light on the proceedings in the matter, quotations are given at some length. The first case was the *Laurence* of Leith, plundered by English pirates in May 1580 on her return voyage from Bordeaux. Some of the well-known merchants of Edinburgh, who were interested parties, the skipper and some of his crew appeared before the Council, and "becaus it wes complenit be the saidis merchantis that ane greitt quantitie of thair guidis and merchandice in the said schip wes pilleit and reft the said vayage be certane Inglis pirats and siclyke the said skipper, clerk and company declaret that thai had thair claithis pilleit be the saidis pirats, thairfor the saidis haill merchandis, skipper, clerk and company wer content and consentit that ane generall scatt and extent wer sett upoun the haill guidis and schip according to thair wairing, conforme to the act of burrowes maid thairanent." The inquiry began in June and went on till September, when the persons charged with the work propounded a difficulty to the Council. They said they were in doubt "gif the said scatt suld be sett upoun the wairing onelie without respect of the fraucht and chairges, or gif the said frawcht and chairges suld be deduceit and comptit in the wayring." The Council answered the inquiry by a ruling, which they declared was to be applicable in future in all such cases. They found that "conforme to the acts of burrowes the said scatt or contributioun be sett according to the wairing of the frank, pund greitt or dolour, and every ane to be ane utheris brother and ilk persoun . . . to pay his awin frawcht and chairges swa that the same be nocht respectet, comptet nor deduceit in the wayring at the setting of the said scatt." This is a clear case of the Town Council's powers as regards the other burghs. The inquiry dragged on, for, as the records put it, those ostensibly engaged upon it were "partly absent furth of this burgh, slaw and negligent." Towards the middle of October the Council, "willing to put ane small end to the said cause," summoned all parties concerned and gave judgment. As the proceedings were long, a summary must suffice. They found the value of the cargo and ship to amount to 3498 li. 10s., and the losses to 1399 li. 13s. 3d. assessed by them as 40 per cent. of the whole. Having settled the total amount of damages, the Council proceeded to inquire into and assess the value of each man's interest in the ship and cargo and the amount of their losses. Most of the ventures were small, with the exception of two merchants and the skipper and crew. The latter had a venture of their own, being fifteen tuns of wine, at 634 li. 10s. ; William Macmathe, merchant, had thirty-two tuns of wine, at 1287 li. ; and Thomas

Paterson had fourteen "polkis" of woad and "fyve thowsand rosseit," valued at 305 li. 6s. 8d. There is no mention of an owner, so that the skipper must have owned the ship, valued at 943 li. After the list had been completed, the magistrates laid down the sums payable by those who had lost least, or not at all, to those who had lost all or a part. Macmathe, having lost only seven tuns of his goods, was obliged to pay 36 li. 19s. 7d. ; Paterson, who had lost heavily, received 190 li. 10s. 1d. ; the skipper and crew had only lost half a tun of wine and paid up 232 li. 17s. 11d. ; the ship had lost 143 li. worth of sails, anchors and tackle, and had to pay 234 li. 12s. to the others, who had been more unfortunate. Possibly the proceedings were given in great detail, because, as the Council had stated, the method of valuation was intended to establish a precedent.

A year later the *Hugoneit* of Leith met with storms on her voyage from Dieppe and the master was forced to lighten ship. The setting of the scatt was accompanied with less delay, for three months later the result was given by the Council. The losses were not so great as those of the *Laurence*, amounting to 512 li. 15s. 7d., from a cargo worth 6835 li. 18s. The exchange was estimated at 16s. to the franc, and the loss to $13\frac{1}{2}$d. in the franc. The part of this scatt which is most remarkable, is the number of merchants and the smallness of their respective ventures. There were forty-three who had a share in the cargo, of whom twenty-eight lost

Trading Losses

nothing, three lost all that they had, being small amounts, valued at 40s. in each case. The rest lost amounts varying from the largest sum of 96 li. to the smallest, 8s. Among other known names is that of John Macmorane, reputed one of the wealthiest Edinburgh burgesses, who escaped without loss of his parcel of goods, valued at 40s., but had to pay 2s. 4d. for the relief of less fortunate brethren. There were also two women with shares in the cargo, one the widow of a freeman and unnamed, the other apparently trading under her own name.

Much might still be gathered from the Burgh Records and other sources to show the part played by Edinburgh merchants in foreign trade. The narrative given in these pages covers only a few years of the history of the burgh, with the intention of indicating some of the Council's and merchants' activities on their own behalf and on behalf of the other burghs, for the economic history of Scotland has not yet been written.

INDEX

303

Index

Index

Index

Index

Index

Index

Index

Index

311

Index

Index

Index

Index

Trade Incorporations, 57

Trades, 180
  apothecaries, 260, 263
  baxters or bakers, 65, 260, 261
  bonnetmakers, 65, 260, 268
  brewers or maltmen, 264
  candlemakers, 262
  confectioner or "sukkerman," 262, 263
  cooks, 260, 262, 264, 265
  cordiners, 65, 75
  fleshers, 7, 65, 260, 261
  furriers, 65, 260, 261
  goldsmiths, 65, 260, 264, 265
  hammermen, guild of, 65, 260
  masons, 65, 77, 260
  milkmen, 265
  shoemakers, 260, 265
  skinners, 65, 260, 261, 264, 265, 268
  smiths, 260
  surgeons, 65, 260
  tailors, 65, 74, 260, 261
  taverners and innkeepers, 260, 264
  waulkers, 65, 260
  weavers, 65, 260
  wrights, 65, 260

Trades' councillors, 182
  convener of, 40, 65, 180, 200
  deacon convener of, 181, 182, 195, 199
  deacons of, 63, 179, 182, 183, 188

Treasury, The, 238, 241, 250, 254

Trinity College, 79, 296
  Provosts of, Sir Edward Boncle, 179

Trinity College Hospital, 5, 6
  Masters of, 8

Trinity College, Cambridge, 112

Trinity Even, 154, 272, 273

Trot, Betty, 12

Trout, 7

"Tuilzie," A, 64, 68

Tweedies of Drummelyier, 210

UNION of the Crowns, 221

Urquhart and Fyvie, Alexander, Lord, 80

" Usurpation," The, 81

VANE, SIR HARRY, 80

View of the Financial Affairs of the City of Edinburgh, 227, 243

Villages. *See* Police Commissioners, Districts

WALES, PRINCE OF, ALBERT EDWARD, 87

War Department, 33, 44, 45

Wards. *See* Police Commissioners, Districts, and, 193, 194
  after Act of 1833 : — Calton, Broughton, St Bernard's, St George's, St Stephen's, St Luke's, St Andrew's, Canongate, St Giles', St Cuthbert's, George Square, St Leonard's, Newington, 200
  additional, after Extension Act of 1896 : — Portobello West Ward, Middle Ward, East Ward, 200
  after Act of 1900 : — Calton, Canongate, Newington, Morningside, Merchiston, Gorgie, Haymarket, St Bernard's, Broughton, St Stephen's, St Andrew's, St Giles', Dalry, George Square, St Leonard's, Portobello, 200
  after Extension Act of 1920 :— South Leith, West, Central, Liberton, Colinton, Corstorphine and Cramond, 200, 201

Watching and warding, 267

Water of Forth, 99
  of Leith. *See* Leith

Watson, Mr Boog, *Roll of Edinburgh Burgesses*, 66

315

Index

PRINTED IN GREAT BRITAIN BY OLIVER AND BOYD, EDINBURGH.